FREUD ON INSTINCT AND MORALITY

FREUD

on Instinct
and Morality

DONALD C. ABEL

State University of New York Press

Published by
State University of New York Press, Albany

For information, address State University of New York
Press, State University Plaza, Albany, N.Y., 12246

Library of Congress Cataloging-in-Publication Data

Abel, Donald C., 1948–
    Freud on instinct and morality / Donald C. Abel.
        p.   cm.
    Bibliography: p.
    Includes index.
    ISBN 0-7914-0024-7.   ISBN 0-7914-0025-5 (pbk.)
    1. Instinct. 2. Instinct—Moral and ethical aspects. 3. Freud,
Sigmund, 1856–1939. I. Title.
BF685.A24   1989
150.19′52—dc 19   88-28247
                                                              CIP

10 9 8 7 6 5 4 3 2 1

TO MY PARENTS

Contents

Acknowledgments

I wish to express my gratitude to all those who have given me their counsel and encouragement in the writing of this book. Their kind and helpful criticism of earlier drafts has made for a much better book. I am especially grateful to Reginald E. Allen, Kenneth Seeskin, and Kenneth I. Howard of Northwestern University, Diane Legomsky of St. Norbert College, Michael A. Wallach of Duke University, Robert Hogan of the University of Tulsa, and Timothy Gould of Metropolitan State College, Denver. Special thanks to Carola F. Sautter, my editor at the State University of New York Press, who has been highly supportive from the beginning and helped steer the manuscript through several revisions. Finally, I wish to thank Robert L. Horn, Dean of St. Norbert College, for generous financial assistance from the Faculty Publications Fund, and Peggy Schlapman for her able secretarial assistance.

In addition, grateful acknowledgment is given to the following publishers for permission to quote from their works:

Sigmund Freud Copyrights Ltd, The Institute of Psycho-Analysis, and The Hogarth Press for permission to quote from *The Standard Edition of the Complete Psychological Works of Sigmund Freud*, translated and edited by James Strachey.

Basic Books, Inc., Publishers, for permission to reprint excerpts from *Three Essays on the Theory of Sexuality*, by Sigmund Freud, Translated and Newly Edited by James Strachey, Copyright © 1962 Sigmund Freud Copyrights Ltd; and excerpts from

Acknowledgments

Collected Papers, Vol. 4, by Sigmund Freud, Authorized Translation under the supervision of Joan Riviere. Published by Basic Books, Inc., by arrangement with The Hogarth Press Ltd and The Institute of Psycho-Analysis, London.

Unwin Hyman Ltd for permission to reprint excerpts from *Complete Introductory Lectures on Psycho-Analysis*, by Sigmund Freud, translated and edited by James Strachey.

Alfred A. Knopf, Inc., for permission to reprint excerpts from *Moses and Monotheism*, by Sigmund Freud, translated by James Strachey, copyright © 1939 by Alfred A. Knopf.

Liveright Publishing Corporation for permission to reprint excerpts from *Introductory Lectures on Psychoanalysis* by Sigmund Freud, Translated and Edited by James Strachey, by permission of Liveright Publishing Corporation. Copyright © 1966 by W. W. Norton & Company, Inc. Copyright © 1965, 1964, 1963 by James Strachey. Copyright 1920, 1935 by Edward L. Bernays.

W.W. Norton & Company, Inc., for permission to reprint excerpts from *The Ego and the Id* by Sigmund Freud, Translated by Joan Riviere, Revised and Edited by James Strachey, by permission of W. W. Norton & Company, Inc. Copyright © 1960 by James Strachey.

Civilization and Its Discontents by Sigmund Freud, Translated and Edited by James Strachey, by permission of W. W. Norton & Company, Inc. Copyright © 1961 by James Strachey.

New Introductory Lectures on Psychoanalysis by Sigmund Freud, Translated and Edited by James Strachey, by permission of W. W. Norton & Company, Inc. Copyright © 1965, 1964 by James Strachey. Copyright 1933 by Sigmund Freud. Copyright renewed 1961 by W. J. H. Sprott.

An Outline of Psycho-Analysis by Sigmund Freud, Translated and Edited by James Strachey, by permission of W. W. Norton & Company, Inc. Copyright 1949 by W. W. Norton & Company, Inc. Copyright © 1969 by The Institute of Psychoanalysis and Alix Strachey.

Beyond the Pleasure Principle by Sigmund Freud, Translated and Edited by James Strachey, by permission of W. W. Norton & Company, Inc. Copyright © 1961 by James Strachey.

Introduction

On January 30, 1927, Freud wrote to the psychologist Werner Achelis, "You seem to be familiar with my attitude toward philosophy (metaphysics) . . . . I not only have no talent for it but no respect for it either. In secret—one cannot say such things aloud—I believe that one day metaphysics will be condemned as a nuisance, as an abuse of thinking" (Freud 1960, pp. 374–375). In a letter to his friend Max Eitingon dated April 22, 1928, Freud declared, "Philosophers no doubt believe that . . . they are contributing to the development of human thought, but every time [they have] a psychological or even a psychopathological problem" (quoted in Jones 1957, p. 140).

Freud sees a radical difference between philosophy and psychoanalysis. Philosophy is a "world view," whereas psychoanalysis is a science. Freud defines a world view as an intellectual system that claims to solve "all the problems of our existence uniformly on the basis of one overriding hypothesis." The hypothesis comes from "revelation, intuition or divination." Science, by contrast, limits itself to "the intellectual working over of carefully scrutinized observations," and does not claim to have all the answers to life's problems. Science produces genuine knowledge, but world views do not. To accept the doctrines of a philosophical (or religious or artistic) world view is "to lay open the paths which lead to psychosis" (Freud 1933a [1932], SE 22:158–160).

If psychoanalysis differs from philosophy, it is for Freud even farther removed from moral philosophy. Moral philosophy deals with values, while psychoanalysis concerns itself simply with facts. A world view "directs . . . thoughts and actions by precepts which it lays down with its whole authority," while science "is content to investigate and to establish facts" (pp. 161–162).

The thesis of this book is that despite Freud's low opinion of philosophy and despite his claim that psychoanalysis avoids value judgments, psychoanalytic theory does contain a moral philosophy. By a moral philosophy I mean a relatively comprehensive set of principles that guides a person in the living of his or her life. Freud's set of moral principles is implicit rather than explicit, but still quite real. I shall argue that Freud's moral philosophy is best characterized as individualistic hedonism.

It is ironic that, inasmuch as he was a moral philosopher, Freud fulfilled his original intellectual ambition. At the beginning of his career (thirty years before he made the disparaging remarks about philosophy quoted in the opening paragraph), Freud confided to his friend Wilhelm Fliess, "I most secretly nourish the hope of arriving [through medical practice] at my initial goal of philosophy. For that is what I wanted originally" (letter of January 1, 1896, in Freud 1985, p. 159). A few months later he explained to Fliess, "As a young man I knew no other longing than for philosophical knowledge, and now I am about to fulfill it as I move from medicine to psychology" (letter of April 2, 1896, p. 180; see Freud 1935a, SE 20:72).

My claim that psychoanalysis contains a moral philosophy rests on the assumption that what a person should do, most fundamentally, is live in a way that fulfills his or her nature. To be moral, then, for Freud would be to fulfill (i.e., to live in consonance with) one's human nature, psychoanalytically understood.

Freud himself never says outright that human beings should live in a way that fulfills their nature, and the argument of this book does not depend on his acceptance of this assumption. But his general approach to psychotherapy indicates that he does accept it. The aim of psychoanalytic therapy is to cure neurotic patients by helping them understand their human nature and enabling them to live within their psychic means (see Freud 1919a [1918], SE 17:159). To regain health, the patient must live in a way consonant with his or her own nature, and not simply adopt the particular ideals the analyst may hold. Freud rejects the notion that analysts should try to form patients into their own image: when the analyst plays the role of teacher and mentor in therapy, "the patient should be educated to liberate and fulfil his own nature, not to resemble [the analyst]" (p. 165; see Freud 1916–17 [1915–17], SE 16:433–434). If the analyst encourages a patient to adopt lofty ideals beyond the capacity of his or her human nature, the analyst is likely to defeat the purpose of therapy by inducing a return of neurosis (Freud 1912e, SE 12:118–119).

According to Freud we are all neurotic to some degree, and therefore the goal of understanding our nature and living according to this knowledge presumably holds for everyone, not just for those undergoing therapy. "An unbroken chain bridges the gap between the neuroses in all their manifestations and normality . . . . We are all to some extent hysterics" (Freud 1905d, SE 7:171). Everyone has dreams, and since "dreams are themselves a neurotic symptom," it follows that "the difference between neurosis and health holds only during the day" (Freud 1916–17 [1915–17], SE 15:83, 16:456). Moreover, faulty actions ("Freudian slips") are performed "by both normal and neurotic people . . . [and] deserve to be rated as symptoms" (Freud 1910a [1909], SE 11:37–38). Indeed, one of Freud's better-known works is entitled *The Psychopathology of Everyday Life* (Freud 1901b). By living in a way that fulfills our nature, we become better able to avoid neurosis and attain happiness, which is what we all seek most fundamentally (Freud 1930a [1929], SE 21:76).

Since Freud's moral theory flows from his view of human nature, the first step in studying that theory is to determine what his view of human nature is. Throughout his writings Freud makes many and various assertions about the workings of human nature. Where in his writings should we look for an account of the essential nature of human beings?

First, we should turn to his theoretical and speculative works rather than to his case studies. While the latter contain brilliant insights into the workings of the psyches of individual patients, the explanatory framework for these insights is to be found mainly in the theoretical and speculative writings. Second, within these works it is best to focus on Freud's various models of the human psyche. For it is in his formulation of these models that Freud reveals his most basic thinking about human nature.

Freud posits three distinct yet overlapping models of the mind. The 'dynamic' model portrays mind as a site of interacting forces (Freud 1916-17 [1915-17], SE 15:67). The 'economic' model views the psyche as a mechanism for controlling the flow and distribution of energy (Freud 1926f, SE 20:265-266). The 'topographic' or 'systematic' model describes mental events in terms of their relationships to regions or systems of the mind. In Freud's earlier writings, the three regions or systems are the unconscious, preconscious, and conscious (Freud 1915e, SE 14:172-176); later they are replaced by the id, ego, and superego (Freud 1926f, SE 20:266).

Matters would be simplified if there were a single notion underlying and unifying these three psychic models. Fortunately, there is such a concept: instinct. With regard to the dynamic model, Freud states that the interacting forces "are originally in the nature of *instincts*" (Freud's emphasis). The energy that powers the psyche in the economic model is located in "the mental representatives of the instincts." And in the later formulation of his third model, Freud posits the id as the most basic element of the mind; the ego and superego develop from the id. The id, in turn, is "the repository of the instinctual impulses" (pp. 265-266).

The concept of instinct, then, is the key to understanding Freud's theory of human nature. Freud himself affirms this point: "Psychological—or, more strictly speaking, psycho-analytic—investigation shows . . . that the deepest essence of human nature consists of instinctual impulses which are of an elementary nature, which are similar in all men and which aim at the satisfaction of certain primal needs" (Freud 1915b, SE 14:281). Nine years later he explains that "the theory of instincts is the most important . . . portion of psycho-analytic theory" (Freud 1905d [1924 add.], SE 7:168, n. 2). In his last major theoretical work Freud states that "the core of our being . . . is formed by the obscure *id* . . . . Within this id the organic *instincts* operate" (Freud 1940a [1938], SE 23:197, Freud's emphasis).

Since Freud's theory of instincts constitutes the basis of his implicit moral philosophy, Part One of this book presents a detailed examination of that theory. In chapter 1, "The Concept of Instinct," I argue that Freud has three different notions of instinct, and that these are best synthesized in the concept of an instinct as something that exerts pressure on the mind to cause a person to act in a way that reduces inner tension.

The next three chapters of Part One recount the three stages in Freud's continuing effort to provide a satisfactory classification schema for the diverse array of human instincts. Chapter 2, "The Sexual and Ego Instincts," explains why Freud, in his early period (1899–1914), considers the sexual instinct and the ego instinct the two fundamental categories of human impulse, and discusses which specific instincts are to be included in each category. Chapter 3, "The Problem of Narcissism," deals with the transitional stage in Freud's instinct classification theory (1914-1920). During this time Freud realizes that his analysis of narcissism undermines any clear distinction between the sexual and ego instincts, but nonetheless refuses to abandon his dualistic theory. In chapter 4, "The Life and Death Instincts," I explain how Freud, in his final period (1920–1939), replaces his initial dualism of the sexual and ego impulses with the more radical dualism of the life and death impulses.

In the chapters discussing Freud's earlier and later classification theories, I explore the connection between each of the two sets of instincts and the general definition of instinct arrived at in the first chapter. I conclude that none of the instincts of either theory (the sexual and ego instincts, the life and death instincts) really fits Freud's general concept of what an instinct is.

Part Two makes explicit the moral philosophy contained in Freud's view of human nature (i.e., in his theory of instincts). Chapter 5, "Freud's Implicit Moral Theory," shows that both Freud's general concept of instinct and his sexual-ego classification schema imply a moral theory of individualistic hedonism.

According to that theory, all pleasure, and only pleasure, is intrinsically good; pleasures differ only in quantity, not in quality; an individual should maximize his or her own pleasure; and certain fundamental conflicts exist between the individual and society. In this chapter I also explain that, due to the problematic nature of the death instinct, Freud's life-death classification schema implies no specific moral theory.

Chapter 6, "Individualism and Group Psychology," discusses Freud's writings on group psychology and examines their compatibility with Freud's individualism. I argue that despite certain nonindividualistic strands in Freud's account of group psychology, his account remains fundamentally individualistic.

This book, I should point out, is limited to an analysis of the moral philosophy implicit in Freud's theory of instincts; it does not explain in any systematic way Freud's personal views on modern-day morality. His basic critique is well known: modern morality places unreasonable restrictions on instinctual satisfaction and requires individuals to live psychologically beyond their means—frequently driving them to neurosis. These restrictions apply to both sexual impulses (see Freud 1908d, " 'Civilized' Sexual Morality and Modern Nervous Illness") and aggressive impulses (see Freud 1930a [1929], *Civilization and Its Discontents*). Freud believed that "certain instinctual impulses, with whose suppression society has gone too far, should be permitted a greater amount of satisfaction" (Freud 1925e [1924], SE 19:220).

Yet Freud was no antinomian or libertine: he assures us that "psycho-analysis has never said a word in favour of unfettering instincts that would injure our community" (p. 219). As Philip Rieff observes in *Freud: The Mind of the Moralist*, "No more compulsively moral man has ever explored the compulsiveness of morality" (Rieff 1979, pp. xxi–xxii). Whether Freud's personal moral beliefs are consistent with his moral philosophy of individualistic hedonism, I shall let the reader decide.

There exists already a vast body of literature on Freud. No one, however, has previously examined in detail the moral philosophy implicit in Freud's doctrine of "the deepest essence of human nature": the instincts. Given Freud's pervasive influence on contemporary culture and self-understanding, there is much to be gained by an articulation of his implied moral theory.

Freud's Theory
of Instincts

The Concept
of Instinct

To explore the concept of instinct,[1] Freud remarks in 1910, is to delve into "the chaos of the obscurer processes of the mind" (Freud 1911c [1910], SE 12:74). Five years later he explains that although the notion of instinct is "somewhat obscure," it is nonetheless "indispensable to us in psychology" (Freud 1915c, SE 14:118). After devoting considerable thought to the concept of instinct over the next five years, Freud declares that it is "at once the most important and the most obscure element of psychological research" (Freud 1920g, SE 18:34). He repeats this judgment in 1924: "The theory of instincts is the most important but at the same time the least complete portion of psycho-analytic theory" (Freud 1905d [1924 add.], SE 7:168, n. 2).

The central importance of the notion of instinct to psychoanalytic theory led Freud to propose various hypotheses about instincts over the years, despite the extraordinary difficulty of the topic. He was never overly confident of these hypotheses. In 1932, for example, he speaks of his doctrine of instincts as a mythology: "The theory of instincts is so to say our mythology. Instincts are mythical entities, magnificent in their indefiniteness. In our work we cannot for a moment disregard them, yet we are never sure that we are seeing them clearly" (Freud 1933a [1932], SE 22:95; see Freud 1933b [1932], SE 22:211).

Freud speculates about both the concept of instinct as such and the proper ways of classifying the various instincts. He spends more time on the latter topic than the former, largely because of the usefulness in therapeutic practice of categorizing a patient's different kinds of impulses. The former topic is, of course, logically prior; one must know what is to count as an instinct before one classifies an impulse as an instinct. The present chapter analyzes Freud's concept of instinct. The three remaining chapters of Part One discuss the three stages in Freud's attempt to classify the instincts.

Freud's most extensive and systematic treatment of the notion of instinct is found in his 1915 essay "Instincts and Their Vicissitudes." Before proceeding to an analysis of this essay, however, it will be helpful to discuss two principles with which Freud presupposes his reader is familiar: the constancy principle and the pleasure principle.

Freud first formulated his principle of constancy in 1892: "The nervous system endeavours to keep constant something in its functional relations that we describe as the 'sum of excitation'" (Freud 1940d [1892], SE 1:153). The nervous system, Freud explains more fully in 1915, strives to master incoming stimuli:

> The nervous system is an apparatus which has the function of getting rid of stimuli that reach it, or of reducing them to the lowest possible level; or which, if it were feasible, would maintain itself in an altogether unstimulated condition . . . .
> Let us assign to the nervous system the task—speaking in

general terms—of *mastering stimuli.* (Freud 1915c, SE 14:120, Freud's emphasis)

The nervous system strives to reduce or eliminate stimulation because an organism always experiences stimulation (excitation, tension) as unpleasurable, and every organism always tries to avoid unpleasure (pain).[2]

Freud holds that the mind developed in the course of evolution as an extension of the nervous system. Hence the human mind (or, to use Freud's preferred term, the mental apparatus) has the same aim as the nervous system of every organism: the removal of inner tension. "We have recognized our mental apparatus as being first and foremost a device designed for mastering excitations which would otherwise be felt as distressing or would have pathogenic effects" (Freud 1914c, SE 14:85). "The ultimate aim of mental activity . . . [is] the task of mastering the amounts of excitation (mass of stimuli) operating in the mental apparatus and of keeping down their accumulation which creates unpleasure" (Freud 1916–17 [1915–17], SE 16:375).

Freud also holds that the reduction of unpleasure is always correlative with the production of pleasure. He makes this claim in his first published description of the phenomenon of pleasure: "The accumulation of excitation . . . is felt as unpleasure and . . . a diminution of excitation . . . as pleasure" (Freud 1900a [1899], SE 5:598). Sixteen years later he makes this point again: "Unpleasurable feelings are connected with an increase and pleasurable feelings with a decrease of stimulus" (Freud 1915c, SE 14:120–121). And in 1920 he equates "an avoidance of unpleasure" with "a production of pleasure" and explains that "unpleasure corresponds to an *increase* in the quantity of excitation and pleasure to a *diminution*" (Freud 1920g, SE 18:7, 8, Freud's emphasis.)

The constancy principle designates the general rule governing all nervous systems; the "pleasure principle" is Freud's term for the rule governing the operation of the nervous system's extension: the mental apparatus. In his *Introductory Lectures on Psycho-Analysis* Freud asks "whether in the operation of our mental apparatus a main purpose can be detected." He answers that "it seems as though our total mental activity is directed toward achieving pleasure and avoiding unpleasure—that it is automatically regulated by the *pleasure principle*" (Freud 1916–17 [1915–17], SE 16:356, Freud's emphasis).

A few years later, in *Beyond the Pleasure Principle*, Freud presents the doctrine of the pleasure principle with greater conviction:

> In the theory of psycho-analysis we have no hesitation in assuming that the course taken by mental events is automatically regulated by the pleasure principle. We believe, that is to say, that the course of events is invariably set in motion by an unpleasurable tension, and that it takes a direction such that its final outcome coincides with a lowering of that tension—that is, with an avoidance of unpleasure or a production of pleasure. (Freud 1920g, SE 18:7)

Because the elimination of unpleasure always goes hand in hand with the creation of pleasure, Freud sometimes calls the pleasure principle the "unpleasure principle" (e.g., Freud 1900a [1899], SE 5:600), and sometimes the "pleasure-unpleasure principle" (e.g., Freud 1926f, SE 20:266). He first uses the term "pleasure principle" in 1911, explaining that it is simply a shortened form of "pleasure-unpleasure principle" (Freud 1911b, SE 12:219).

An important corollary of the pleasure principle is the reality principle. Experiencing how things work in the real world teaches a person that is not always advisable to reduce inner tension immediately: to do so may bring greater unpleasure in the long run. For example, to satisfy one's desire for certain types of foods may eventually lead to poor health. So one may forgo these foods in order to avoid the pain of poor health. To do so is to follow the reality principle, "which at bottom seeks to obtain pleasure, but pleasure which is assured through taking account of reality, even though it is pleasure postponed and diminished" (Freud 1916–17 [1915–17], SE 16:357).

To obey the reality principle, therefore, is not to give up the search for pleasure, but to seek it more intelligently. In Freud's words, the reality principle "does not abandon the intention of ultimately obtaining pleasure, but it nevertheless demands and carries into effect the postponement of satisfaction, the abandonment of a number of possibilities of gaining satisfaction and the temporary toleration of unpleasure as a step on the long indirect road to pleasure" (Freud 1920g, SE 18:10).

In "Instincts and Their Vicissitudes" Freud uses his notions of the constancy principle and the pleasure principle to formulate a definition of instinct. In fact, he ends up giving not one but three definitions, apparently unaware of the conceptual shifts in his discussion.

Freud begins his essay by defining an instinct as a certain type of stimulus. Stimuli are of two kinds: those that impinge on the nervous system and those that affect the mental apparatus. The former are "applied to the living tissue (nervous substance) *from* the outside [and] discharged by action *to* the outside" (Freud 1915c, SE 14:118, Freud's emphasis). The organism responds to these stimuli in accordance with the constancy principle; it uses muscular action to withdraw from the stimuli. To give an example (not Freud's), a hot coal touches a dog's skin and the dog reacts by quickly moving away from the coal.

Stimuli of the second type are also physical in nature, but impinge on the mind. A human being responds to these stimuli in accordance with the pleasure principle; he or she tries to eliminate or at least reduce the physically caused mental tension. Some stimuli affecting the mental apparatus can be effectively handled through muscular action. Freud gives the example of a strong light falling on the eye. This stimulus can be dealt with through physical movement — one can turn one's head away. There are other kinds of stimuli affecting the mind, however, that cannot be handled through muscular activity. Take Freud's example of the mental tension caused by hunger. A hungry person cannot alleviate the irritation of the mucous membrane of the stomach by mere physical movement. It is this second kind of stimulus impinging on the mind that Freud calls an instinct (p. 118 and n. 2).

Freud explains the difference between instincts and those noninstinctual stimuli that affect the mind as follows:

> In the first place, an instinctual stimulus [i.e., an instinct] does not arise from the external world but from within the organism itself. For this reason . . . different actions are necessary in order to remove it. Further, all that is essential in a [noninstinctual] stimulus is covered if we assume that it operates with a single impact, so that it can be disposed of by a single expedient action . . . . An instinct, on the other hand, never operates as a force giving a *momentary* impact but always as a *constant* one. (p. 118, Freud's emphasis)

Freud sums up his discussion thus far by defining the "essential nature" of instincts in terms of their three main attributes, namely, "their origin in sources of stimulation within the organism and their appearance as a constant force . . . [and the fact that] no actions of flight avail against them" (p. 119).

Freud's statement that an instinct is a constant force calls for comment. For some stimuli that affect the mind and are not removed by flight do not seem to be constant. Consider Freud's example of hunger: do not the irritation of the mucous membrane and the resulting sitmulus on the mind subside for a time after food is eaten and digested? By describing an instinct as a constant stimulus, Freud must mean that it occurs regularly and frequently (like hunger), rather than irregularly and occasionally (like bright light on the eye). Ernest Jones thus seems correct in interpreting "constant" here as meaning "fairly constant" (Jones 1936, p. 277).

Freud describes the impact of noninstinctual stimuli on the mind as momentary. But is it not possible for some such stimuli, e.g., a bright light, to be more than momentary? Furthermore, could not some of these stimuli, e.g., ordinary daily sounds or smells, occur regularly and frequently?

Freud's distinction between constant and momentary stimuli seems to refer more to the place of origin of a stimulus than to its duration. Hunger can be described as a (fairly) constant stimulus because it originates in the organism's stomach and follows the organism wherever it goes; a bright light is momentary in the sense that it originates outside the organism and can (at least ordinarily) be avoided.

The three chief attributes of instincts are, then, closely related. The origin of instincts "in sources of stimulation within the organism" accounts for the appearance of instincts as "a constant force," and these two features of instincts imply the third, that "no actions of flight avail against them" (Freud 1915c, SE 14:119).

According to this initial discussion of the nature of instinct in "Instincts and Their Vicissitudes," an instinct is a kind of stimulus—specifically, a stimulus impinging on the mind (rather than on the nervous system) that originates in the organism, produces a fairly constant force, and cannot be avoided through mere physical movement.

Shortly after defining an instinct as a type of stimulus, Freud in his essay writes that "an 'instinct' appears to us . . . as the psychical representative of the stimuli originating from within the organism and reaching the mind" (pp. 121–122). Several paragraphs later he writes similarly that certain stimuli are "represented in mental life by an instinct" (p. 123).

Whereas Freud initially defined an instinct as a stimulus, he here defines it as the *representative* of a stimulus. A stimulus is a physical entity; even when a stimulus impinges on the mind rather than the body, the stimulus is viewed by Freud as something physical. This is clear from the two examples Freud gives of stimuli affecting the mind: a strong light (noninstinctual stimulus) and an irritation of the mucous membrane of the stomach (instinctual stimulus). That which *represents* a stimulus, on the other hand, is a mental entity, a "psychical representative." That Freud considers such a representative to be nonphysical is apparent from his definition of "instinctual representative" as an "idea" in two works published along with "Instincts and Their Vicissitudes" (Freud 1915d, SE 14:152; Freud 1915e, SE 14:177).

In "Instincts and Their Vicissitudes" Freud puts forth a third view of the nature of instinct. Shortly after defining an instinct as a mental representative, he goes on to explain the notion of pressure:

By the pressure of an instinct we understand its motor factor, the amount of force or the measure of the demand for work which it represents. The characteristics of exercising pressure is common to all instincts; it is in fact their very essence. (Freud 1915c, SE 14:122)

This passage begins by explaining an attribute of an instinct (something it *has*), and ends up by stating the essence of an instinct (what it *is*). And since the statement of essence is a definition, Freud is here giving a third definition of instinct: an exerter of pressure. More specifically, an instinct is something that exerts pressure on the mind to make a "demand for work," i.e., a demand that the mind direct the organism to act (in accordance with the pleasure principle) in a way that will reduce or eliminate tension.

Freud's third definition differs importantly from the first two in that it avoids assigning to instinct an ontological status. A stimulus is not said here to be either something physical (first definition) or something mental (second definition); it is simply viewed as an exerter of pressure, and as such could be physical or mental or, perhaps, something in-between. This third definition only states what an instinct *does*; it does not attempt to specify what it essentially *is*.

Before discussing the reasons behind the shifts in Freud's ways of viewing an instinct, it will be helpful to survey briefly the definitions of instinct in Freud's other writings, and to correlate these to the three definitions in "Instincts and Their Vicissitudes."

Freud's first published definition of instinct appears in a work written in 1910: "We regard instinct as . . . the psychical representative of organic forces" (Freud 1911c [1910], SE 12:74).[3] This notion of instinct directly corresponds to the second definition in "Instincts and Their Vicissitudes."

Freud gives a similar definition in the 1915 edition of his *Three Essays on the Theory of Sexuality*: "the psychical representative of an endosomatic, continuously flowing source of stimulation." A few lines later, however, he presents a notion of instinct parallel to the third definition in "Instincts and Their Vicissitudes":

"a measure of the demand made upon the mind for work" (Freud 1905d [1915 add.], SE 7:168).

In his 1915 article "Repression," Freud explains that in one kind of repression "the psychical (ideational) representative of the instinct [is] denied entrance into the conscious" (Freud 1915d, SE 14:148). Here Freud draws a distinction between an instinct and its mental representative; an instinct is apparently assumed to be a stimulus (first definition in "Instincts and Their Vicissitudes") rather than the mental representative of that physical stimulus (second definition). He reaffirms this distinction several pages later: "We have dealt with the repression of an instinctual representative, and by the latter we have understood an idea or group of ideas that is cathected[4] with a definite quota of psychical energy . . . coming from an instinct" (p. 152).

In "The Unconscious," also published in 1915, Freud again conceives of an instinct as a stimulus (first definition) rather than as its psychic representative (second definition): "An instinct can never become an object of consciousness—only the idea that represents the instinct can. Even in the unconscious, moreover, an instinct cannot be represented otherwise than by an idea" (Freud 1915e, SE 14:177).

Freud's definition of instinct in *Beyond the Pleasure Principle* (1920) parallels the second definition in "Instincts and Their Vicissitudes." Instincts are said to be "the representatives of all the forces originating in the interior of the body and transmitted to the mental apparatus" (Freud 1920g, SE 18:34).

In his *New Introductory Lectures on Psycho-Analysis* of 1933, Freud conceives of an instinct both as a stimulus (first definition in "Instincts and Their Vicissitudes") and an exerter of pressure (third definition). First, he states that "an instinct is distinguished from a [noninstinctual] stimulus by the fact that it arises from sources of stimulation within the body, that it operates as a constant force and that the subject cannot avoid it by flight" (Freud 1933a [1932], SE 22:96). (Earlier in these lectures he rejected the view of an instinct as a mental representative [second definition in "Instincts and Their Vicissitudes"] by differentiating an instinct [understood as a stimulus] from its "psychical expression" [p. 73].) Second, Freud defines an instinct as "a certain quota of energy which presses in a particular direction" (p. 96; see Freud 1909b, SE 10:140–141).

Freud's final discussion of the concept of instinct appears in the posthumously published *Outline of Psycho-Analysis*. Here all three definitions put forth in "Instincts and Their Vicissitudes" reappear. Freud distinguishes an instinct from its "psychical expression" (Freud 1940a [1938], SE 23:145), thereby implying that an instinct is a stimulus (first definition). He also depicts instincts as mental representatives: they "represent the somatic demands upon the mind" (second definition). And earlier in this same paragraph he says that instincts are "forces which we assume to exist behind . . . tensions" (third definition) (p. 148).

Freud seems to be unaware that there are three different notions of instinct operative in his writings on the subject. He moves from one notion to the next—sometimes within the scope of a single paragraph—without trying to reconcile the differing conceptions. The fundamental reason for Freud's vacillation in "Instincts and Their Vicissitudes" and other works seems to be his uncertainty about the ontological status of instincts. He remarks in 1910 that an instinct lies "on the frontier-line between the somatic and the mental" (Freud 1911c [1910], SE 12:74), and makes the same point again three years later (Freud 1913j, SE 13:182) and two years after that (Freud 1915c, SE 14:122). Because an instinct, in some respects, seems to be a physical entity and, in other respects, something mental, and because of his assumption that an instinct must be either physical or mental, Freud at times views an instinct as a stimulus (something physical), and at times as the representative of a stimulus (something mental). Hence the first two different and incompatible definitions of instinct (see Strachey, SE 14:113; Chessick 1980, p. 258).

Freud's third definition has the advantage of saying what Freud wanted to say about the function of instincts in the human organism without specifying their ontological status. By describing an instinct as an "exerter of pressure" Freud can leave open the question whether this exerter of pressure is something physical or something mental. And for the practical purposes of therapy, it seems sufficient simply to say what an instinct *does*, without involving oneself in the ontological question of what an instinct really *is*.

I take Freud's third definition of instinct, therefore, to be the most representative of his thought on the topic. One can, moreover, expand this definition so that it makes reference to both the physical and the mental aspects of instinct (its somatic origin and its pressure on the mind), thereby incorporating the essential points from Freud's first and second definitions. In the expanded version, the third definition would be: something that exerts pressure on the mind to cause the organism to act in a way that will eliminate or reduce the tension caused by endosomatic and fairly constant stimuli.

Since this definition is formulated in terms of the function an instinct plays in a person's life, it is apposite to examine here Freud's various remarks about the goal of instincts.

In two of his works Freud identifies the goal of an instinct as the psychological state of satisfaction. In "Instincts and Their Vicissitudes" he writes, "The aim of an instinct is in every instance satisfaction" (Freud 1915c, SE 14:122). He repeats this point in *The Question of Lay Analysis*: "What, then, do [the] instincts want? Satisfaction" (Freud 1926e, SE 20:200). The way to achieve satisfaction is to eliminate tension: "Satisfaction . . . can only be obtained by removing the state of stimulation at the source of the instinct" (Freud 1915c, SE 14:122).

In his *New Introductory Lectures*, however, Freud views the goal of an instinct not as the feeling of satisfaction but as the physical process that produces satisfaction: the aim "invariably remains the bodily change which is felt as satisfaction" (Freud 1933a [1932], SE 22:96). So while the removal of tension in the body leads to the mental state of satisfaction, the satisfaction is not itself the goal. The physical process that was a means to the feeling of satisfaction in "Instincts and Their Vicissitudes" becomes itself the goal of an instinct in the *New Introductory Lectures*.

It is somewhat surprising that Freud's (expanded third) definition of instinct makes no mention of satisfaction, but speaks only of reducing tension. The reason for the omission seems to be Freud's thesis that the physical process of tension reduction and the mental state of satisfaction are inseparable; the removal of tension in an organism always causes pleasure, and is the only cause of pleasure. For Freud, to say that an instinct strives to eliminate tension is virtually equivalent to saying that it strives for satisfaction—"virtually" equivalent because, strictly speaking, the two differ as cause and effect.

Freud's definition of instinct makes no mention of pleasure for the same reason that it makes no mention of satisfaction: the removal of tension always causes pleasure, and is the only cause of pleasure. The mind always functions according to the pleasure principle, and pleasure is achieved by following the instinctual desire to reduce tension. In fact, "pleasure" and "satisfaction" seem to be synonymous terms for Freud.

The connection between tension reduction and pleasure (satisfaction) is so close that at times Freud seems to equate them. For example, he states in *Beyond the Pleasure Principle* that the pleasure principle regulates the course of mental events in such a way that "its final outcome coincides with a lowering of tension — that is, with an avoidance of unpleasure or a production of pleasure" (Freud 1920g, SE 18:7).

According to the analysis presented in this chapter, then, the definition of instinct most faithful to Freud's thought is the expanded version of the third definition of "Instincts and Their Vicissitudes": something that exerts pressure on the mind to cause an organism to act in a way that will reduce the tension caused by endosomatic and fairly constant stimuli. And the physical process of reducing stimulation causes a feeling of pleasure (satisfaction) in the organism. It is this notion of instinct that I shall take as normative for Freud when, in the following three chapters, I discuss the three stages of Freud's attempt to devise a comprehensive schema for classifying the multifarious human instincts.

2

The Sexual and
Ego Instincts

After discussing the nature of instinct in "Instincts and Their Vicissitudes," Freud turns his attention to the problem of classifying the various human impulses that qualify as instincts. Are there certain basic instincts under which all instinctual impulses can be categorized?

> What instincts should we suppose there are, and how many? There is obviously a wide opportunity here for arbitrary choice. No objection can be made to anyone's employing the concept of an instinct of play or of destruction of or gregariousness, when the subject-matter demands it . . . . Nevertheless, we should not neglect to ask ourselves whether instinctual motives like these . . . admit of further dissection . . . so

that only primal instincts — those which cannot be further dissected — can lay claim to importance. (Freud 1914c, SE 14: 123–124)

Freud's views about which instincts are primal fall into three stages. In his first period (1899–1914) he maintains confidently that the two basic and irreducible human impulses, under which all others can be subsumed, are the sexual instinct and the ego instinct. Then he begins to doubt the adequacy of this theory because of certain implications of his analysis of narcissism. In this middle period (1914–1920) he uneasily holds on to his sexual-ego dualism, largely because he cannot find a more plausible dualism with which to replace it. Freud then hits upon the idea of a death instinct, and in his final period (1920–1939) maintains that life and death are the primordial impulses. (See the Appendix for a discussion of other interpretations of the stages in Freud's instinct classification theory.)

This chapter examines the instinct classification theory of Freud's early period; the following chapters treat the middle and late periods. I begin by surveying the pertinent works of the years 1899–1914, showing that for Freud during this time the sexual and ego instincts are the basic human impulses. I then investigate the meaning of the elusive terms "sexual instinct" and "ego instinct." Finally, I relate Freud's concepts of the sexual and ego instincts to the general definition of instinct formulated in chapter 1.

Freud's belief that the sexual and ego impulses are the fundamental kinds of human instinct is already evident in 1899, the year he finished writing *The Interpretation of Dreams*. The central thesis of this major work is that every dream has a meaning, and that the meaning is the mental fulfillment of some wish of the dreamer: "When the work of interpretation has been completed, we perceive that a dream is the fulfilment of a wish" (Freud 1900a [1899], SE 4:121). More precisely, "a dream is the (disguised) fulfilment of a (suppressed or repressed) wish" (p. 160; see pp. 122–133).

Human beings, of course, have all sorts of wishes. But Freud's analyses of dreams (his own and others') very frequently pointed to hidden sexual desires. During the day, sexual wishes are often repressed because they conflict with one's moral and personal ideals. At night, however, one's psychic "censor" is less rigorous and permits some sexual wishes to be represented in dreams—though even these wishes often must assume disguises in order to get past the censor (pp. 135, 277–278).

In his 1909 edition of *The Interpretation of Dreams* Freud notes, "The more one is concerned with the solution of dreams, the more one is driven to recognize that the majority of the dreams of adults deal with sexual material and give expression to erotic wishes" (Freud 1900a [1909 add.], SE 5:396). He returns to this point in the 1911 edition:

> No one who accepts the view that the censorship is the chief reason for dream-distortion will be surprised to learn from the results of dream-interpretation that most of the dreams of adults are traced back by analysis to *erotic wishes*. A great many . . . dreams . . . which show no sign of being erotic in their manifest content, are revealed by the work of interpretation in analysis as sexual wish-fulfilments. (Freud 1900a [1911 add.], SE 5:682, Freud's emphasis)

The fundamental psychic conflict Freud portrays in *The Interpretation of Dreams* occurs between the impulse for sexual pleasure and the impulse for preserving one's self-image and self-respect. Freud rarely uses the term "instinct" in this early work, but will later identify these impulses as the sexual and ego instincts.

In *The Interpretation of Dreams* Freud views these two instincts as basic not only because they help explain dreams, but also because he is convinced that every neurosis is traceable to the repression, during childhood, of a sexual impulse by an ego impulse (pp. 605–606).

In 1905 Freud published his *Three Essays on the Theory of Sexuality*, his most comprehensive treatment of the sexual instinct. Here he exlores not only the sexual instinct, but also those impulses that can oppose it. He notes that "the sexual instinct has to struggle against certain mental forces which act as resistances, and of which shame and disgust are the most prominent" (Freud 1905d, SE 7:162). Neuroses are once again attributed to the repression of the sexual instinct by (what will later be called) the ego instincts.

> All my experience shows that . . . psychoneuroses are based on sexual instinctual forces . . . . The sexual life of the persons in question is expressed . . . [in] symptoms . . . . Those symptoms are substitutes—transcriptions as it were—for a number of emotionally cathected mental processes, wishes and desires, which, by the operation of a special psychical procedure (repression), have been prevented from obtaining discharge in psychical activity that is admissible to consciousness. (pp. 163–164)

In the *Three Essays* Freud appeals to certain biological studies to support his thesis that the sexual instinct cannot be reduced to other (namely, ego) instincts. These studies suggest that there exists throughout the body a sexual substance that chemically breaks down and causes sexual excitation when affected by the appropriate stimulus (p. 216, n. 1; see Freud 1915c, SE 14:125).

Freud's 1907 paper, "Obsessive Actions and Religious Practices," contrasts the sexual instinct with impulses to act selfishly: "The formation of religion . . . seems to be based on the suppression . . . of certain instinctual impulses. These impulses, however, are not, as in the neuroses, exclusively components of the sexual instinct; they are self-seeking, socially harmful instincts" (Freud 1907b, SE 9:125). This instinct to seek one's own good at the expense of others is "egoistic" in the ordinary meaning of the term; it is what Freud will later identify as the ego instinct.

It is in his essay of 1910 on "The Psycho-Analytic View of Psychogenic Disturbance of Vision" that Freud first uses the term "ego-instincts" (*Ichtriebe*, more literally "I-instincts" or "self-instincts"). The passage in question draws a clear contrast between the sexual and the ego instincts:

We have discovered that every instinct tries to make itself effective by activating ideas that are in keeping with its aims. These instincts are not always compatible with one another; their interests often come into conflict . . . . A quite specially important part is played by the undeniable opposition between the instincts which subserve sexuality, the attainment of sexual pleasure, and those other instincts, which have as their aim the self-preservation of the individual—the ego-instincts. As the poet [Schiller] has said, all the organic instincts that operate in our mind may be classified as 'hunger' or 'love'. (Freud 1910i, SE 11:213–215)

Freud goes on to explain how the conflict between the sexual and the ego instincts can lead to neurosis:

'Neuroses' are derived from the many different ways in which [the] processes of transformation in the sexual component may miscarry. The 'ego' feels threatened by the claims of the sexual instincts, and fends them off by repressions; these, however, do no always have the desired result, but lead to the formation of dangerous substitutes for the repressed . . . . From these . . . phenomena . . . there emerge what we call the symptoms of neuroses. (p. 215)

In 1910 Freud calls the sexual-ego categorization a "popular" one, and (as in the *Three Essays*) finds support for this view in biology: "We accept the popular distinction between ego-instincts and a sexual instinct; for such a distinction seems to agree with the biological conception that the individual has a double orientation, aiming on the one hand at self-preservation and on the other at the preservation of the species" (Freud 1911c [1910], SE 12:74).

Freud's 1914 essay, "On Narcissism: An Introduction," marks the end of the first period of Freud's instinct classification theory. For in this essay Freud acknowledges that this analysis of the phenomenon of narcissism raises serious doubts about his previously held thesis that the sexual and ego instincts are primal and irreducible. The essay on narcissism is discussed in the following chapter, since it begins the middle period of Freud's efforts to classify the instincts. Yet the following passage from the essay merits quotation here, since it gives Freud's principal reasons for originally positing his sexual-ego dualism.

> There are various points in favour of the hypothesis of there having been from the first a separation between the sexual instincts and others, ego-instincts, besides the serviceability of such a hypothesis in the analysis of . . . neuroses . . . . In the first place, this distinction corresponds to the popular distinction between hunger and love. In the second place, there are biological considerations in its favour. The individual actually does carry on a two-fold existence: one to serve his own purposes and the other as a link in a chain. . . . Thirdly, we must recollect that all our provisional ideas in psychology will presumably some day be based on an organic substructure. This makes it probable that it is special substances and chemical processes which perform the operations of sexuality. (Freud 1914c, SE 14:78)

In Freud's early period, then, the two equiprimordial impulses, under which all human impulses can be categorized, are the sexual and ego instincts. But what precisely does Freud mean by "sexual instinct" and "ego instinct"? The former term is especially problematic, and requires an extended discussion.

Freud makes it clear that in psychoanalysis the concept of what is sexual "comprises far more" than it does in popular understanding (Freud 1910k, SE 11:222). He explains that "sexual" is a broader term than "genital," since it "includes many activities that have nothing to do with genitals" (Freud 1940a [1938], SE 23:152). But exactly how much broader is it? The closest Freud comes to giving an explicit answer to this crucial question seems to be the following statement: "We use the word 'sexuality' in the same comprehensive sense as that in which the German language uses the word *lieben* ['to love']" (Freud 1910k, SE 11:223). But this explanation of the meaning of "sexual" is hardly satisfactory, since the extension of the *lieben* (like the English "love") is itself unclear.

Unfortunately, Freud gives us no explicit criterion we can use to determine whether or not a particular impulse is sexual in nature. But there is an indirect way to discern what Freud means by "sexual instinct." This way lies in analyzing the notion of sexuality implicit in his discussions of sexual *activity*.

A sexual instinct may be described in a preliminary way as an impulse to engage in sexual activity. And since Freud has more to say about sexual activity than about the sexual instinct itself (though he defines neither term), it will be helpful to examine some of his writings on sexual activity.

Freud's most detailed theoretical treatment of sexual activity is his *Three Essays on the Theory of Sexuality*. The second of these essays, "Infantile Sexuality," thoroughly examines the sexual activities of infants and young children. This essay makes it clear that "sexual" is for Freud a broader term than "genital": children do not engage in foreplay or intercourse, yet according to Freud many of their activities are sexual.

In "Infantile Sexuality" Freud states that although many diverse infantile activities are sexual, sensual sucking is a particularly clear "sample of the sexual manifestations of childhood" and that a close examination of this phenomenon reveals "the essential features of infantile sexual activity" (Freud 1905d, SE 7:179, 181). Sensual sucking

> consists in the rhythmic repetition of a sucking contact by the mouth (or lips). There is no question of this procedure being the taking of nourishment. A portion of the lip itself, the tongue, or any part of the skin within reach — even the big toe — may be taken as the object upon which this sucking is carried out . . . . Sensual sucking involves a complete absorption of the attention and leads either to sleep or even to a motor reaction in the nature of an orgasm. It is not infrequently combined with rubbing some sensitive part of the body such as the breast or the external genitalia. Many children proceed by this path from sucking to masturbation. (pp. 179–180)

21

After giving this description of sensual sucking, Freud asserts that "no observer has felt any doubt as to the sexual nature of this activity" (p. 180, n. 2).

What is it that makes sensual sucking, in Freud's view, so obviously sexual? The decisive feature seems to be the pleasure involved—more precisely, pleasure divorced from any useful function. When a child first sucks, it draws milk from its mother's breast. But sensual sucking aims at oral pleasure apart from any goal of nourishment. "It is clear that the behaviour of a child who indulges in thumb-sucking is determined by a search for some pleasure which has already been experienced and is now remembered" (p. 181).

The essay on "Infantile Sexuality" does not say explicitly that the goal of pleasure is what makes sensual sucking a paradigmatic sexual activity. But this view is all but explicitly stated in Freud's discussion of sucking in his *Introductory Lectures on Psycho-Analysis*, and is stated outright in *An Outline of Psycho-Analysis*.

In the *Introductory Lectures* Freud remarks that "when children fall asleep after being sated at the breast, they show an expression of blissful satisfaction which will be repeated later in life after the experience of a sexual orgasm" (Freud 1916–17 [1915–17], SE 16:313). But the similarity between the two pleasures is not by itself enough to establish the sexual nature of sucking at the breast, since sucking has the useful function of providing nourishment. Freud goes on to note, however, that an infant will often suck even when this activity provides no nourishment. It is this feature of sucking that makes it a sensual and a seuxal activity:

> We observe how an infant will repeat the action of taking in nourishment without making a demand for further food; here, then, he is not actuated by hunger. We describe this as sensual sucking, and the fact that in doing so he falls asleep once more with a blissful expression shows us that the act of sensual sucking has in itself alone brought him satisfaction. (p. 313)

Freud returns to the topic of sucking in his *Outline of Psycho-Analysis*, and here makes explicit his view that the distinguishing feature of a sexual activity is that the pleasure of the activity is pursued for its own sake: "The baby's obstinate persistence in sucking gives evidence . . . of a need for satisfaction which . . . strives to obtain pleasure independently of nourishment and for that reason may and should be termed *sexual*" (Freud 1940a [1938], SE 23:154, Freud's emphasis).

Since a sexual instinct is an impulse to engage in sexual activity, we can use the above definition of sexual activity to arrive at a definition of sexual instinct: an impulse to engage in an activity whose pleasure is sought for its own sake (see Freud 1908d, SE 9:188).

This interpretation of the meaning of sexual instinct in Freud is confirmed by an examination of Freud's concepts of a "component sexual instinct" and of an "erotogenic zone." Both notions are first introduced in "The Sexual Aberrations," the first of Freud's *Three Essays*. In this essay Freud analyzes various components of perverse sexual activities. This in turn suggests that the sexual *instinct* has several components: "If perversions admit of analysis . . . , then they must be of a composite nature. This gives us a hint that perhaps the sexual instinct itself may be no simple thing, but put together from components which have come apart again in the perversions" (Freud 1905d, SE 7:162). Freud's first use of the term "component instinct" occurs several pages later, in the same passage where he first defines "erotogenic zone":

> If we put together what we have learned from our investigation of . . . perversions, it seems plausible to trace them back to a number of 'component instincts' . . . . We can distinguish in them a contribution from an organ capable of receiving the stimuli (e.g. the skin, the mucous membrane or a sense organ). An organ of this kind will be described . . . as an 'erotogenic zone'. (pp. 167–168 and p. 168, n. 1)

Reflection on certain sexual perversions reveals that two of the sexual instincts are the impulses for oral and for anal pleasure; the corresponding erotogenic zones are the mouth and the anus (p. 169).

In the second of his *Three Essays*, "Infantile Sexuality," Freud observes that the oral and anal component instincts are operative in children. Children not only take pleasure in sucking; they also delight in anal sensations, as is evidenced by the fact that they sometimes hold back their stool "till its accumulation brings about violent muscular contractions and, as it passes through the anus, is able to produce powerful stimulation of the mucous membrane" (p. 186). A third infantile erotogenic zone is the genitals. Although prepubertal children do not have full orgasms, they feel pleasure when their genitals are handled by another person or by themselves, and likewise feel pleasure when urinating (pp. 187–188).

A child's erotogenic zones are not limited to the oral, anal, and genital regions; a child is, in Freud's well-known phrase, "polymorphously perverse." That is to say, a child can derive pleasure from many different bodily regions (p. 191). In fact, Freud claims in "Infantile Sexuality" that the entire skin and all mucous membranes are potentially erotogenic (p. 183). In "Instincts and Their Vicissitudes," written ten years later, he makes an even broader claim: "We can decide to regard erotogenicity as a general characteristic of all organs" (Freud 1915c, SE 14:84). And in 1938 he asserts simply that "the whole body is an erotogenic zone" (Freud 1940a [1938], SE 23:151).

When Freud introduces the idea of component instincts of erotogenic zones, he does not so much *argue* that these impulses and bodily regions are sexual, as *assume* that they are. For Freud, a component instinct is by definition a component sexual instinct, and an erotogenic zone is by definition a region that gives rise to sexual (erotic) pleasure. The reasoning behind this assumption sheds light on what Freud means by the term "sexual." Let us examine this reasoning.

The striking feature of the oral, anal, and genital regions for Freud is their ability to cause pleasure; indeed, every part of the body is potentially pleasure-producing. And the remarkable thing about the psyche in this regard is its desire to experience pleasure from so many different bodily areas. These observations would warrant the conclusion that every part of the body is *"hedono-genic"* (capable of producing pleasure [*hēdonē*]), and that there are various component *pleasure* instincts. But Freud concludes that every part of the body is *eroto*genic (capable of producing *sexual* pleasure), and that there are various component *sexual* instincts.

What Freud does here is equate pleasure with sexual pleasure. That is to say, he assumes that all pleasure is sexual pleasure. This assumption underlying his discussions of erotogenic zones and component instincts confirms the thesis that by the term "sexual instinct" Freud means an impulse to engage in an activity whose pleasure is pursued for its own sake.

Two passages from Freud's *Three Essays* seem to contradict my contention that it is the potential for pleasure that prompts Freud to label certain bodily regions and certain impulses as sexual. These passages state that nongenital areas of the body can be called sexual because they are analogous to the genitals. Freud writes that the oral and anal orifices "behave in every respect like a portion of the sexual apparatus . . . . In hysteria these parts of the body . . . become the seat of new sensations and of changes in innervation . . . in just the same way as do the actual genitalia under the excitations of the normal sexual processes" (Freud 1905d, SE 7:169). In the second text Freud explains that repression can affect the genital zones, and that then these areas can "transmit their susceptibilty to other erotogenic zones . . . , which then behave exactly like genitals" (pp. 183–184).

In arguing that nongenital regions can be called sexual because of their similarity to the genital region, Freud seems to avoid appealing to pleasure as the distinguishing mark of the sexual. But one may ask for the justification of Freud's assumption that the genitals are the prime instance of an erotogenic zone. If "sexual" is a wider concept than "genital," what makes the genitals paradigmatically sexual? Freud's reason would seem to be that the genitals are the source of the most intense type of pleasure. And just as the impulse to genital activity is a sexual impulse

25

because it strives for pleasure for its own sake, so the impulses to activity involving other parts of the body are sexual because they strive for pleasure for its own sake. So even when Freud explains erotogenic zones and component instincts in terms of their analogy to the genitals, his argument rests ultimately on the notion of pleasure.

In the early period of Freud's instinct classification theory, then, the category of sexual instincts includes all those impulses to perform activities whose pleasure is sought for its own sake.

The other category of impulses in Freud's first period is the ego instinct. What kinds of human desires does Freud intend to include here?

In *The Interpretation of Dreams* and the *Three Essays* the ego instinct is not yet named; it is simply the unspecified set of impulses that can come into conflict with the sexual desires and cause the repression of those desires—the repression sometimes creating neurotic symptoms. These unnamed impulses are, as I have already argued, basically wishes to preserve one's self-respect and self-image. To engage in certain sexual activities, or even to entertain sexual thoughts, conflicts with one's idealized image of oneself—with what is later called the "ego ideal" (Freud 1914c, SE 14:95) or "superego" (*Uber-Ich*, "above-I" or "above-self") (Freud 1923b, SE 19:28).

In 1907 Freud characterizes the impulses opposed to sexual desires as "self-seeking, socially harmful instincts" (Freud 1907b, SE 9:125). So in addition to impulses to maintain one's ego ideal, the ego instinct also includes selfish ("egoistic") impulses.

When Freud introduces the term "ego instincts" in 1910, he describes them as those instincts "which have as their aim the self-preservation of the individual" (Freud 1910i, SE 11:214). "Self-preservation" obviously includes the desire for continued physical existence. But it includes more than this. The ego instincts are those desires that conflict with the sexual instincts, and rarely would a sexual desire endanger one's physical survival. The "self" in "self-preservation" is usually the idealized self rather than the physical self; impulses to preserve one's self-image and self-respect are what oppose sexual desires. Freud's inclusion of the ego ideal in the category of ego instinct is made clear in a 1916 discussion of neurosis: "For a neurosis to be generated there must be a conflict between a person's libidinal [i.e., sexual] wishes and the part of the personality we call his ego, which is the expression of his instinct of self-preservation and which also includes his *ideals* of his personality" (Freud 1916d, SE 14:316, Freud's emphasis).

To sum up this examination of the meaning of ego instinct in Freud's early instinct classification theory: an ego instinct is an impulse to preserve one's physical existence, to enhance one's life selfishly at the expense of others, or to maintain one's idealized self-image. If we understand the term "self-preservation" in the broad Freudian sense, we can define an ego instinct simply as an impulse for self-preservation.

Now that we have workable definitions of both the sexual instinct and the ego instinct, we may turn our attention to the final topic of this chapter. Do the sexual and ego instincts fit the general concept of instinct that Freud presents in "Instincts and Their Vicissitudes"? Is either the sexual or the ego instinct an entity that exerts pressure on the mind in order to cause the organism to act in a way that will eliminate or reduce the tension caused by endosomatic and fairly constant stimuli?

According to this definition of instinct, two conditions must be met if an impulse is to be classified as an instinct: there must be tension caused by an endosomatic and constant stimulus, and there must be pressure exerted on the mind to cause the organism to remove this tension. I shall first discuss the relation of the sexual instinct to these criteria, and then consider the ego instinct.

In the case of the sexual instinct, is there an endosomatic stimulus causing tension in the organism? With regard to impulses to genital activity, the answer seems affirmative: there is a stimulus of some sort, and it can be viewed as arising within the body—although the internal stimulus may itself be triggered by an external stimulus (see Freud 1933a [1932], SE 22:96). The stimulus is also constant, in the sense of occurring regularly.

The sexual instinct, however, includes much more than desires for genital activity; it includes every desire for an activity whose pleasure is sought for its own sake. And it is not obvious

27

that impulses to experience nongenital pleasures always involve tension or, even if they do, that there is an endosomatic and constant stimulus causing that tension. One wonders what the tension-causing stimulus would be in the case of a person's desire to see a beautiful landscape, to know the truth, or to be with a friend. And even if there were stimuli in such cases, the resulting tension would seem to be endopsychic rather than endosomatic. Moreover, the tension would not be constant, even in Freud's sense of the term.

Freud would presumably defend his claim that nongenital desires meet the first criterion for instincts by claiming that desires like those for beauty, truth, and friendship are simply transformations of what originally were desires for genital activity. Here Freud would most likely invoke his theories of sublimation, aim inhibition, reaction formation, etc. But an exposition of these theories (along with a discussion of some of the problems they raise for Freud's theory of the sexual instinct) is best postponed until chapter 5.

There is a second condition an impulse must meet if it is to qualify as an instinct: there must be pressure exerted on the mind to cause the organism to act to eliminate or reduce the endosomatic, constant tension. Do the sexual instincts fulfill this criterion?

If it is true that nongenital sexual impulses do not always involve tension, then clearly it would be false that in the case of all sexual instincts there is pressure exerted on the organism to reduce tension. But let us assume for the moment that nongenital sexual desires do involve tension. Is there pressure to remove the tension?

According to Freud's conception of the sexual instinct, a sexual instinct aims at the experience of pleasure. And according to the pleasure principle, pleasure is experienced through tension reduction: tension is unpleasurable and its removal is pleasurable. These claims lead to problems.

First of all, we do not in fact experience all tension as unpleasurable, and do not always seek to eliminate it. As Richard Chessick notes:

> There is considerable experimental evidence to support the contention that the brain is a stimulus-seeking rather than a

stimulus-avoiding system . . . . Instead of seeking a low-level equilibrium . . . , the brain is continuously active in its need for optimal stimulation. As sensory-deprivation experiments have shown, the brain, instead of welcoming a peaceful state, engages in a veritable frenzy of activity in its search for stimuli and ends up by artificially providing them through fantasies, hallucinations, and so forth. (Chessick 1980, p. 303).

Michael Wallach and Lise Wallach concur:

Stimulus input does not seem to be inherently and originally offensive to the nervous system, flooding it with unwanted excitation. To the contrary, stimulation is necessary for the nervous system's proper functioning. Minimizing stimulation in restricted environments leads to boredom and restlessness and, when kept up long enough, to deteriorization of cognitive processes and hallucinations. (Wallach and Wallach 1983, p. 52)

With regard to specifically genital tension, it seems clear that stimulation itself is frequently pleasurable, and is often sought rather than avoided. For many years Freud's theoretical commitment to the constancy principle and the pleasure principle kept him from acknowledging this obvious fact of human experience. In 1924, however, he acknowledged that genital stimulation—and other kinds as well—can be pleasurable:

[We have] attributed to the mental apparatus the purpose of reducing to nothing, or at least of keeping as low as possible, the sums of excitation which flow in upon it . . . . But such a view cannot be correct . . . . It cannot be doubted that there are pleasurable tensions . . . . The state of sexual excitation is the most striking example . . . , but it is certainly not the only one. (Freud 1924c, SE 19:159–160)

Unfortunately, Freud does not seem to realize that his admission that some tensions are pleasurable requires a major revision of his theory of instincts. Or if he does realize it, he never undertakes such a revision.

Freud's thesis that all sexual instincts aim at reducing tension creates another serious problem for his instinct theory—one that eventually caused him to abandon his sexual-ego classification schema. The problem is that, in the final analysis, *all* instincts (including the ego instincts) seem to be sexual.

Freud defines both an instinct in general and the sexual instinct in particular in terms of their goals: an instinct is something that aims at tension reduction, and the sexual instinct is something that aims at pleasure. But, as I argued in the previous chapter, tension reduction is for Freud simply a means to the end of pleasure. And since Freud conceives of an instinct in terms of its aim, it seems legitimate to define it in terms of its ultimate end (pleasure) rather than its more immediate end (tension reduction). (As we saw, Freud himself at times equates tension reduction with pleasure.) But if all instincts aim at pleasure, then all instincts become sexual. And at this point, the sexual-ego dualism of Freud's early classification theory collapses into a sexual monism.

Such are the chief difficulties that arise when one tries to fit Freud's notion of the sexual instincts to his general definition of instinct. Problems arise as well when one takes up his notion of ego instincts.

According to the first criterion of instinct, if an ego impulse is to qualify as an instinct, there must be tension caused by an endosomatic and constant stimulus. Is there tension present in every impulse to preserve one's physical existence, to enhance one's life at the expense of others, or to maintain one's self-respect and self-image? It seems quite implausible. While there may be tension when an ego instinct comes into conflict with a sexual instinct, e.g., when a desire to maintain one's idealized self-image opposes a desire for a certain form of genital gratification, there would seem to be no tension in the ego instinct *itself*. What sort of tension would there be in the desire, as such, for self-preservation? And even if there were a tension in such a desire, it would seem to be endopsychic rather than endosomatic.

The second criterion is that pressure be exerted on the mind to cause the organism to act to remove the tension. If the ego impulses have no inherent tension, there will of course be no pressure to remove it. But let us suppose that there is such tension. In this case, these impulses would (as we have seen) fall under the category of sexual instincts: they would be aiming at tension reduction, and thereby be aiming ultimately at pleasure—and thus be, by definition, sexual impulses. So once again Freud's instinctual dualism would be reduced to a monistic theory.

Freud himself does not seem to be aware of the instinctual monism that results from trying to fit his concept of a sexual or an ego instinct into his general definition of instinct. The main reason for his lack of awareness seems to be his failure to produce a clear definition of "sexual instinct." But if I am correct in arguing that what Freud implicitly means by this term is an impulse to engage in an activity whose pleasure is sought for its own sake, Freud's thesis that the sexual and ego instincts are equiprimordial and irreducible seems untenable.

Interestingly, in 1914 Freud did begin to question the viability of his instinctual dualism—but for reasons rather different from those outlined above. His doubts stemmed from his analysis of the phenomenon of narcissism: if one can have a sexual impulse toward one's self (ego), the distinction between the sexual and ego instincts becomes blurred. Despite the challenge that narcissism posed for his original instinct classification schema, however, Freud held on to his sexual-ego dualism until he replaced it with a life-death dualism in 1920. This transitional period in Freud's instinct classification theory (1914–1920) is the topic of the following chapter.

3

The Problem
of Narcissism

FREUD'S 1914 essay, "On Narcissism: An Introduction," is rightly judged by James Strachey to be "among the most important of Freud's writings and . . . one of the pivots in the evolution of his views" (Strachey, SE 14:70). The essay is crucial for Freud's instinct classification theory because the concept of narcissism calls into question the soundness of Freud's long-held thesis that the sexual and ego instincts are the two basic and irreducible categories of human impulse. Freud himself calls attention to the apparently monistic implications of his narcissism analysis, but is reluctant to give up his sexual-ego dualism in favor of a single basic instinct. He holds on to his original dualism until 1920, when he postulates a new and more sweeping dualism: the life and death instincts.

Freud speaks of narcissism several times prior to his detailed study of 1914. He first mentions narcissism when discussing male homosexuality in his 1910 revision of the *Three Essays on the Theory of Sexuality*:

> In all the cases we have examined we have established the fact that the future inverts [homosexuals], in the earliest years of their childhood, pass through a phase of very intense but short-lived fixation to a woman (usually their mother), and that, after leaving this behind, they identify themselves with a woman and take *themselves* as their sexual object. That is to say, they proceed from a narcissistic basis, and look for a young man who resembles themselves. (Freud 1905d [1910 add.], SE 7:145, n. 1, Freud's emphasis)

In his second reference to narcissism, Freud explains that the term derives from a figure in Greek mythology:

> [A boy who becomes a homosexual] represses his love for his mother: he puts himself in her place, identifies with her, and takes his own person as a model in whose likeness he chooses the new objects of his love. In this way he has become a homosexual . . . . He finds the objects of his love along the path of *narcissism*, as we say; for Narcissus, according to the Greek legend, was a youth who preferred his own reflection to everything else and who was changed into the lovely flower of that name. (Freud 1910c, SE 11:100, Freud's emphasis)

Freud also mentions narcissism in several other works published prior to "On Narcissism" (e.g., Freud 1912–13, SE 13:88–90, 93, 130; Freud 1913j, SE 13:189), but in none of these passages does he thoroughly analyze the dynamics of this phenomenon; he simply uses the term to denote the choice of oneself as a sexual object.

In the essay "On Narcissism," Freud distinguishes two types of narcissism. In each type a person's sexual energy (libido) is directed toward the self (ego) rather than toward some external object. "Primary narcissism" refers to the libidinal state of an infant at the beginning of its life; all its libido is directed toward itself (Freud 1914c, SE 14:75, 88). "Secondary narcissism" is a possible later development. Shortly after birth, an infant begins to direct its sexual energy away from the self and invest it in external objects. But later on some individuals withdraw their libido from objects and reinvest it in themselves. This redirection of libido to the ego constitutes secondary narcissism (p. 75).

Freud gives a concise description of secondary narcissism in his *Introductory Lectures.* (He here refers to secondary narcissism simply as narcissism, as he often does when it is clear from the context that he is not discussing primary narcissism.)

> The libido, which we find attached to objects and which is the expression of an effort to obtain satisfaction in connection with those objects, can also leave the objects and set the subject's own ego in their place . . . . The name for this way of allocating the libido [is] 'narcissism'. (Freud 1916–17 [1915–17], SE 16:415–416)

Freud's analysis of narcissism led him to posit two forms of libido. "Ego libido" (also called "narcissistic libido" [Freud 1919d, SE 17:209]) is sexual energy that cathects the self, and "object libido" is sexual energy that cathects external objects (Freud 1914c, SE 14:76). Every person has a fixed quantity of libido, and so an increase in the quantity of one of these two forms of libido entails the decrease in the quantity of the other (p. 78).

If Freud's explanation of narcissism is correct, his thesis about the irreducibility of the sexual and ego instincts is suspect. For according to that thesis, the sexual instincts are directed wholly toward objects and the ego instincts wholly toward the ego. But the concept of ego libido blurs the distinction between the sexual and ego instincts: libido is by definition the energy behind the *sexual* instinct, yet ego libido is by definition directed toward the *ego*.

The problem is intensified by the fact that Freud views ego libido as the fundamental form of libido. The ego is the first object of libidinal cathexis (primary narcissism), and even after a person begins to cathect external objects, ego libido remains the basic type of libido. As Freud explains:

> When it [object libido] is withdrawn from objects . . . and is finally drawn back into the ego . . . , it becomes ego-libido once again . . . . Narcissistic or ego-libido seems to be the great reservoir from which the object-cathexes are sent out and into which they are withdrawn once more; the narcissistic libidinal cathexis of the ego is the original state of things, realized in earliest childhood, and is merely covered by the later extrusions of libido, but in essentials persists behind them. (Freud 1905d [1915 add.], SE 7:217–218)

According to Freud's original instinct classification theory, libido is the energy behind the sexual instinct, and "ego interest" (or, more simply, "interest") is the energy the ego instinct (Freud 1914c, SE 14:82–83; Freud 1916–17 [1915–17], SE 16:414). But the theory of ego libido advanced in "On Narcissism" seems to imply that interest is a derivative of libido, and not equiprimordial with it. And if the ego instincts are ultimately energized by a form of libido, and if libido is sexual energy, then the ego instincts turn out to be actually sexual. So there is in fact only *one* basic type of human impulse, the sexual instinct. Freud's sexual-ego dualism collapses into a sexual monism.

It is not really necessary, however, to describe this resulting monism as sexual. For if there is only one basic impulse, it need not be labeled sexual or anything else; it could simply be called "instinct." The energy behind it, in turn, could simply be called "instinctual energy."

In the essay on narcissism, Freud himself candidly acknowledges the challenge his analysis of narcissism raises for his instinctual dualism:

> If we grant the ego a primary cathexis of libido [i.e., if we grant that libido is first invested in the ego], why is there any necessity for further distinguishing a sexual libido from a non-sexual energy of the ego-instincts [viz., interest]? Would

not the postulation of a single kind of psychical energy save us all the difficulties of differentiating . . . ego-libido from object-libido? . . . To be asked to give a definite answer to [this] question must occasion perceptible uneasiness in every psycho-analyst. (Freud 1914c, SE 14:76–77)

Despite his awareness of the difficulties confronting his sexual-ego instinct classification theory, Freud continues to support this theory in his middle period: he maintains that libido and interest are irreducible, and that, correlatively, the sexual and ego instincts are irreducible. After making the remarks just quoted, Freud proceeds to give four reasons for retaining his sexual-ego dualism: the theory is useful in understanding and treating neuroses; common opinion attests that love and hunger are the basic human impulses; biological studies indicate that an individual seeks not only its own ends, but is the carrier of a potentially immortal germ plasm; and other biological research suggests that organisms possess special sexual substances and chemical processes. Freud admits that psychoanalytic work may eventually lead to a better instinct classification schema, but points out that "so far, this has not happened" (pp. 78–79).

In "Instincts and Their Vicissitudes," written one year later, Freud again defends his sexual-ego schema. He reiterates the first reason given in "On Narcissism," therapeutic utility:

I have proposed that two groups of . . . primal instincts should be distinguished: the *ego*, or *self-preservative*, instincts and the *sexual* instincts . . . . The occasion for this hypothesis arose in the course of the evolution of psychoanalysis . . . , [which] showed that at the root of all [neuroses] there is to be found a conflict between the claims of sexuality and those of the ego. It is always possible that an exhaustive study . . . may oblige us to alter this formula and to make a different classification of the primal instincts. But for the present we do not know of any such formula. (Freud 1915c, SE 14:124, Freud's emphasis)

How strong are the four reasons given in "On Narcissism" for holding on to a sexual-ego dualism in light of the challenge posed by the analysis of narcissism? With regard to the first argument, even if one grants that all neuroses are caused by a conflict between sexual and ego impulses, one could still hold that both types of impulses are derivatives of one primordial instinct. It is not evident that a derivative dualism would be any less useful in psychotherapeutic practice than an irreducible sexual-ego dualism.

The second reason given is that common opinion asserts that love and hunger are basic instincts. But in deciding complex theoretical issues, it seems inappropriate for depth psychology (as Freud often calls psychoanalytic theory) to give much weight to a popular distinction—if indeed it *is* a popular distinction.

The third and fourth reasons adduced in "On Narcissism" consist of the findings of certain biological studies. Irrespective of the validity of those studies, one should note that Freud is ordinarily reluctant to appeal to other sciences when attempting to establish psychoanalytic hypotheses; to do so seems to compromise the independence of psychoanalysis as a science. In fact, shortly after presenting his third and fourth reasons, Freud avows, "I try in general to keep psychology clear from everything that is different in nature from it, even biological lines of thought" (Freud 1914c, SE 14:78–79).

Since none of these explicitly acknowledged reasons explains adequately Freud's continued allegiance to his original instinct classification theory, we should perhaps look for some more fundamental reason. The decisive reason, I suggest, is Freud's deeply held conviction that the mind is a battleground of two equiprimordial and opposing forces. Freud refuses to adopt a derivative dualism because to hold that the sexual and ego forces stem from one basic instinct is to undermine the radical nature of psychic conflict.

The importance of viewing the mind as a site of conflict is evident in all three periods of Freud's instinct theory. In the opening paragraph of *The Interpretation of Dreams* (early period) Freud writes, "I shall . . . endeavour to elucidate the processes to which the strangeness and obscurity of dreams are due and to deduce from those processes the nature of the psychical forces by whose concurrent or mutually opposing action dreams are generated" (Freud 1900a [1899] SE 4:1). In his "Analysis of a Phobia in a Five-Year-Old Boy" (also early period), Freud remarks that "the emotional life of man is in general made up of pairs of contraries . . . Indeed, if it were not so, repressions and neuroses would perhaps never come about" (Freud 1909b, SE 10:113). In his *Introductory Lectures* (middle period) Freud tells his audience, "Without . . . conflict there is no neurosis . . . . Our mental life is, as you know, perpetually agitated by conflicts which we have to settle" (Freud 1916–17 [1915–17], SE 16:349). Finally, in an article written in 1922 (late period), he notes that "psycho-analysis early became aware that all mental occurrences must be regarded as built on the basis of an interplay of the forces of the elementary instincts" (Freud 1923a [1922], SE 18:255). As Daniel Yankelovich and William Barrett observe, "Conflict is probably the key notion throughout all of Freud's thinking . . . . In all of Freud's most far-reaching theories, one basic human experience is pitted against another" (Yankelovich and Barrett 1970, p. 29).

The mind for Freud is a battleground, and he seems simply to assume that the battle is waged between two fundamental and irreducible categories of impulses. The a priori nature of this claim can be seen in three passages from the essay "On Narcissism." In each passage Freud admits that in the given situation one cannot actually differentiate more than one type of instinct or instinctual energy, but nonetheless goes on to assert that there must be two kinds of instinct or energy present.

The first text concerns primary narcissism, the situation in which the infant's instinctual energy is invested in its ego. Rather than draw the seemingly obvious conclusion that during this period there is just one kind of energy, Freud declares that there is simply a practical difficulty in distinguishing sexual energy (libido) from ego energy (interest): "As regards the differentiation of psychical energies, we are led to the conclusion that to begin with, during the state of [primary] narcissism, they exist together and that our analysis is too coarse to distinguish between them; not until there is object-cathexis is it possible to discriminate a sexual energy . . . from an energy of the ego-instincts'' (Freud 1914c, SE 14:76).

Eleven pages later Freud admits that there is no apparent difference between the sexual and the ego instincts in infants, and responds by asserting that, nonetheless, there *must* be two opposing types of impulse: "The sexual instincts are at the outset attached to the satisfaction of the ego-instincts; only later do they become independent of these" (p. 87).

The third text occurs in a discussion of the castration complex theory, Freud's theory that boys have anxiety about being castrated and that girls want to have a penis. Freud admits that in this complex one cannot separate the sexual and ego instincts, but instead of concluding that only one type of instinct is involved, he takes it as a priori true that both types are present: "In the particular field of the castration complex, [psychoanalytic research] allows us to infer the existence of an epoch and a psychical situation in which two groups of instincts, still operating in unison and inseparably mingled, make their appearance as narcissistic interests" (p. 92).

In the middle period of his instinct classification theory, then, Freud maintains his original sexual-ego dualism, despite the fact that his analysis of narcissism seems to imply an instinctual monism. One gets the impression that Freud would be willing to give up his sexual-ego theory if he could replace it with a new version of dualism—one that would allow the fusion of the sexual and ego impulses that seems to constitute the phenomenon of narcissism. And this impression is correct: six years after publishing "On Narcissism" Freud subsumes (most of) the sexual and ego instincts under a newly postulated "life instinct," and proposes a "death instinct" as its opponent. This new instinctual dualism of Freud's late period (1920–1939) is the subject of the final chapter of Part One.

4

The Life and Death Instincts

T HE publication of *Beyond the Pleasure Principle* in 1920 marks the beginning of the final stage of Freud's attempt to classify the instincts. Here Freud proposes a bold new theory that allows for the original unity of the sexual and ego instincts while still preserving an instinctual dualism. Freud accepts the previously troubling implication of his 1914 analysis of narcissism that the sexual and ego instincts are not irreducibly distinct, and sets forth a new theory that puts (most of) both the sexual and ego instincts in the new category of the "life instinct." He is able to maintain a dualism by postulating a "death instinct" as the equiprimordial opponent of the life instinct. Freud explains that his new life-death classification schema is more radically dualistic than his previous sexual-ego category: "Our views have from the first been *dualistic*, and to-day they are even more definitely dualistic than before—now that we describe the opposition as being, not between ego-instincts and sexual instincts but between life instincts and death instincts" (Freud 1920g, SE 18:53, Freud's emphasis).

This chapter begins with a discussion of the more problematic of these two new categories, the death instinct. Then I take up the life instinct. Finally, I examine how well the life and death instincts fit Freud's general conception of what an instinct is.

The psychological phenomenon that led Freud to posit the existence of a death instinct was the human tendency to repeat past experiences—more specifically, the tendency observable in some people to repeat an unpleasurable experience even though the repetition promises to bring more unpleasure than pleasure. What struck Freud about this "repetition compulsion" is its independence from the pleasure principle. As I explained in chapter 1, according to the pleasure principle all mental functioning is governed by the aim of avoiding unpleasure or, equivalently for Freud, experiencing pleasure. In 1920 Freud concludes that the repetition compulsion lies (to quote the title of the book) "beyond the pleasure principle."

To ground his hypothesis of a repetition compulsion, Freud cites a number of cases. Some of his neurotic patients relived certain experiences "which include no possibility of pleasure, and which can never, even long ago, have brought satisfaction even to instinctual impulses which have since been repressed" (p. 20). And Freud knew some nonneurotics who would keep repeating some unpleasurable pattern, e.g., acting toward others in a way that invited betrayal or abandonment (p. 22). Freud found further evidence for the existence of a repetition compulsion in people who had recurring dreams of some past traumatic event. Freud remarks that when the mind produces such dreams it operates "independent[ly] of . . . the purpose of gaining pleasure and avoiding unpleasure" (p. 32).[1] From such examples Freud finds the "courage to assume that there really does exist in the mind a compulsion to repeat which overrides the pleasure principle . . . . Enough is left unexplained [by other psychic mechanisms] to justify the hypothesis of a compulsion to repeat" (pp. 22–23).

Freud goes on to claim that the repetition compulsion is "more instinctual" than the pleasure principle and that the manifestations of the repetition compulsion "exhibit to a high degree an instinctual character" (pp. 23, 35). Could it be that every instinct is characterized by a compulsion to repeat, that every instinct seeks to bring an organism back to the way things were at an earlier time?

> How is the predicate of being 'instinctual' related to the compulsion to repeat? At this point we cannot escape a conclusion that we may perhaps have come upon the track of a universal attribute of instincts and perhaps of organic life in general . . . . *It seems, then, that an instinct is an urge inherent in organic life to restore an earlier state of things.* (p. 36, Freud's emphasis)

Freud decides to carry to its logical conclusion his hypothesis that all instincts aim at restoring an organism to an earlier state. Applying this hypothesis to the evolution of organisms, one can infer that when external forces affected an organism and made it more complex, the organism's internal forces (its instincts) tried to bring it back to its former, simpler stage of development. Furthermore, the hypothesis suggests that when external forces first transformed inanimate matter into a living substance, the new substance possessed an instinct to return to its original, inorganic state. According to this line of reasoning, Freud explains, the ultimate aim of an organism would be to die:

> It is possible to specify [the] final goal of all organic striving . . . It must be . . . an initial state from which the living entity has at one time or another departed and to which it is striving to return by the circuitous paths along which its development leads . . . . *'The aim of all life is death'.* (p. 38, Freud's emphasis)

If death is the ultimate aim of life, an organism's instincts for self-preservation would be simply "the myrmidons of death";

their goal would be only to make sure "that the organism shall follow its own path to death, and to ward off any possible ways of returning to inorganic existence other than those which are immanent in the organism itself" (p. 39).

Such are the logical implications Freud draws from his supposition that the compulsion to repeat is a characteristic of all instincts. But the hypothesis itself, Freud points out, is false. There are some instincts that do not strive to return an organism to an earlier state, e.g., the instincts that direct the activity of its reproductive cells. These instincts aim at life, not death. Freud explains that these cells have a certain independence from the organism in which they reside; they seek each other out, unite, and form a new organism that in turn has independent reproductive cells of its own:

> The whole path of development to natural death is not trodden by *all* the elementary entities which compose . . . the higher organisms . . . . The germ cells . . . separate themselves from the organism as a whole . . . . Under favourable conditions, they begin to develop . . . and in the end once again one portion of their substance pursues its development to a finish [i.e., death], while another portion harks back once again as a fresh residual germ to the beginning of the process of development. (p. 40, Freud's emphasis)

Freud's term for "the instincts which watch over the destinies of these elementary organisms that survive the whole individual" is "the sexual instincts." These instincts aim not only at life, but, through repeated reproduction, at a kind of immortality: "These germ-calls . . . work against the death of the living substance and succeed in winning for it what we can only regard as potential immortality" (p. 40).[2]

While the sexual instincts do not strive for death, all other instincts do. Freud calls these nonsexual instincts, appropriately enough, the "death instincts" (p. 44). He succinctly defines the death instincts as those impulses "which seek to lead what is living to death" (p. 46).

In works subsequent to *Beyond the Pleasure Principle*, Freud claims that the death instinct (as well as the life instinct) is operative on every level of human life—from the individual cell up through complex organisms like human beings. The death instinct is "active in every particle of living substance" (Freud 1923b, SE 19:41); it "cannot fail to be present in every vital process" (Freud 1933a [1932], SE 22:107); it is "at work in every living creature and is striving to bring it to ruin and reduce life to its original condition of inanimate matter" (Freud 1933b [1932], SE 22:211). This broad claim seems to be a revision (unacknowledged by Freud) of the theory proposed in *Beyond the Pleasure Principle* that the reproductive cells aim only at life.

The death instinct manifests itself primarily as an impulse to self-destruction. But this impulse can be diverted away from the organism itself and directed toward other beings:

> As a result of the combination of unicellular organisms into multicellular forms of life, the death instinct of the single cell can successfully be neutralized and . . . diverted on to the external world . . . . The death instinct would thus seem to express itself—though probably only in part—as an instinct of destruction directed against the external world and other organisms. (Freud 1923b, SE 19:41)

Freud goes on to explain that this diverting of the death impulse in a multicellular organism toward external beings is accomplished "through the instrumentality of a special organ . . . , the muscular apparatus" (p. 41). In the case of the human organism, the death instinct is partly diverted to the external world in the form of aggression, partly fused with the sexual instincts, and partly works toward its original goal of self-destruction (p. 54).

In his essay "Why War?," Freud draws attention to the fact that an organism saves its own life at the expense of other beings: "The death instinct turns into the destructive instinct [i.e., destructive of others] when, with the help of special organs, it is directed outwards, on to objects. The organism preserves its own life, so to say, by destroying an extraneous one" (Freud 1933b

[1932], SE 22:211). Freud's theory, in short, is that impulses of destruction or aggression (the two terms are synonymous for Freud; see Freud 1923a [1922], SE 18:258; Freud 1930a [1929], SE 21:121–122) can be "trace[d] back to the original death instinct of living matter" (Freud 1937c, SE 23:243).

One of the advantages of Freud's life-death dualism over his earlier sexual-ego theory is that it provides a more likely niche for the aggressive impulses. In his early and middle periods, Freud does not seem sure whether to place these impulses within the sexual or the ego category. An examination of some of Freud's main statements on aggression in his early and middle periods points to a serious problem for a sexual-ego dualism.

Freud draws a connection between aggression and sadism in the *Three Essays on the Theory of Sexuality*:

> As regards . . . sadism, the roots are easy to detect in the normal. The sexuality of most male human beings contains an element of *aggressiveness*—a desire to subjugate; the biological significance of it seems to lie in the need for overcoming the resistance of the sexual object by means other than the process of wooing. Thus sadism would correspond to an aggressive component of the sexual instinct which has become independent and exaggerated. (Freud 1905d, SE 7:157–158, Freud's emphasis)

What Freud does not say here is whether aggression is to be subsumed *wholly* under the sexual instinct.

Later on in the *Three Essays* Freud links aggression with cruelty. He classifies cruelty as a component sexual instinct, but remarks that "the fundamental psychological analysis of this instinct has . . . not yet been satisfactorily achieved" (p. 193). Nonetheless, Freud proposes the hypothesis that "the impulses of cruelty arise from sources which are in fact independent of sexuality, but may become united with it at an early stage" (p. 193, n. 1). The implication is that aggression has a nonsexual origin, i.e., that it originates in the ego instinct.

In his 1915 revision of the *Three Essays* Freud replaces the above hypothesis with the claim that the cruelty impulse "arises from the instinct for mastery" (Freud 1905d [1915 add.], SE 7:193). This claim is repeated in the *Introductory Lectures*: "An instinct for mastery . . . easily passes over into cruelty" (Freud 1916–17 [1915–17], SE 16:327). But what of the mastery instinct itself? Is it to be considered a sexual or an ego instinct? Freud, as far as I know, never answers this question.

In a case study published in 1909, Freud makes the interesting suggestion that aggressiveness is a factor in all instincts, i.e., in both sexual and ego impulses. In the context of discussing Alfred Adler's theory that aggression is an instinct separate from the sexual and ego instincts, Freud writes: "I cannot bring myself to assume the existence of a special aggressive instinct alongside of the familiar instincts of self-preservation and of sex . . . . Adler has mistakenly promoted into a special and self-subsisting instinct what is in reality a universal and indispensable attribute of *all* instincts" (Freud 1909b, SE 10: 140–141, Freud's emphasis). Freud's suggestion here has some merit, but it seems to compromise his commitment to an unambiguously dualistic basis for psychic conflict and for psychic functioning in general.

At the end of "Instincts and Their Vicissitudes" Freud links hate (a phenomenon closely related to the instinct of aggression, though hate itself is not an instinct but an "attitude" [Freud 1915c, SE 14:137]) with the ego instinct: "The true prototypes of the relation of hate are . . . derived . . . from the ego's struggle to preserve and maintain itself . . . . [Hate] always remains in an intimate relation with the self-preservative instincts" (pp. 138–139). But it is not clear whether the terms "prototype" and "intimate relation" are meant to imply that hate is subsumed entirely under the ego instinct. Nor does Freud explain the precise relation between hate and aggression.

The question of where to locate the problematic aggressive and destructive impulses is apparently solved by Freud's introduction of the death instinct. For these impulses, which do not fit neatly into either the sexual or the ego category, do seem to fall naturally under the heading of this primal instinct. (There is a theoretical difficulty, however, in Freud's claim that an organism's death instinct can be "diverted" to external objects; the problem is discussed later in this chapter.)

The other primal instinct in Freud's 1920 classification theory is the life instinct. Freud first uses the term "life instincts" when giving his explanation (summarized above) of how the reproductive cells are an exception to the hypothesis that all instincts try to return an organism to an earlier stage of development—ultimately to the inanimate state. The impulses that guide the activities of the reproductive cells "constitute the group of sexual instincts . . . . They are the true life instincts. They operate against the purpose of the other instincts, which leads . . . to death" (Freud 1920g, SE 18:40).

While the reproductive cells are the primary locus of the life instincts, these instincts in fact permeate every living creature. The life instinct, like the death instinct, is "active in every particle of living substance" (Freud 1923b, SE 19:41). Freud emphasizes the wide domain of the life instinct by calling it "Eros," the ancient Greek term for love or desire. The life instinct is "Eros, the preserver of all things," that which "seeks to force together and hold together the portions of living substance" (Freud 1920g, SE 18:52, 60, n. 1). Freud explains that "the libidinal, sexual or life instincts . . . are best comprised under the name of *Eros*; their purpose [is] to form living substance into ever greater unities, so that life may be prolonged and brought to higher development" (Freud 1923a [1922], SE 18:258, Freud's emphasis). With regard to the human race, Eros strives "to combine single human individuals, and after that families, then races, peoples and nations into one great unity, the unity of mankind" (Freud 1930a [1929], SE 21:122).[3]

The life instincts are obviously similar to the sexual instincts of Freud's previous classification schema. But does Freud intend to include under the life instinct everything (except the problematic aggressive impulses) that he previously included under the sexual instinct? In other words, does the life instinct include all impulses to engage in activities whose pleasure is sought for its own sake? The answer seems affirmative, for all impulses must fall either under the life or the death instinct, and according to Freud "satisfaction of the death instinct . . . seems not to produce feelings of pleasure" (Freud 1940a [1938], SE 23:154, n. 1).

The life instinct includes the ego (self-preservation) impulses as well. As Freud states in *The Ego and the Id*, the life instinct "comprises not merely the . . . sexual instinct . . . , but also the self-preservative instinct, which must be assigned to the ego and which at the beginning of our analytic work we had good reason for contrasting with the sexual object-instincts" (Freud 1923b, SE 19:40). He makes this point again in *An Autobiographical Study*: "I have combined the instincts for self-preservation and for the preservation of the species [i.e., the ego and the sexual instincts] under the concept of *Eros*" (Freud 1925d [1924], SE 20:57, Freud's emphasis).[4] And when Freud includes "self-preservation" under the life instincts, he presumably intends the term in the broad sense explained in chapter 2—a sense including not only the desire to continue one's physical existence, but also the desires to enhance one's life and to maintain one's idealized self-image.

The new dualism of Freud's late period does more than simply replace one pair of instincts with another; it involves a change in the very notion of instinct. There is a striking difference in tone between Freud's descriptions of the life and death impulses permeating every living being in the cosmos, and his earlier discussions of the impulses in human beings to engage in sexual activity and to preserve their self-respect. Freud himself is aware of his shift from clinical observations to cosmic speculations; he refers to his life-death theory as "so to say our mythology" (Freud 1933a [1932], SE 22:95) and observes that, in the case of the death instinct, the mythology is "not even an agreeable one" (Freud 1933b [1932], SE 22:211).

A fruitful way to examine this important change in Freud's thought is to see how well the life and death instincts fit the general concept of instinct that Freud presented in "Instincts and Their Vicissitudes." In the late period of his instinct classification theory, Freud never officially abandons his 1915 formulation of the nature of instinct. When, in his *New Introductory Lectures* (written in 1932, twelve years after the introduction of his life-death dualism), Freud wants to explain what an instinct is, he simply summarizes the theory of "Instincts and Their Vicissitudes" (Freud 1933a [1932], SE 22:96). He reechoes the theory in *An Outline of Psycho-Analysis*, a work composed in the last year of his life: instincts "represent the somatic demands upon the mind" (Freud 1940a [1938], SE 23:148).

According to "Instincts and Their Vicissitudes," two criteria must be met if an impulse is to qualify as an instinct: there must be tension caused by an endosomatic and constant stimulus, and there must be pressure exerted on the mind to cause the organism to act in a way that will remove the tension. Do the life and death impulses meet these conditions?

The attempt to apply these two criteria to the death instinct is complicated by the difficulty of citing any clear instances of a death impulse. Freud's theory that individual cells strive to return to their original inorganic state is based more on speculation than on evidence. Furthermore, Freud never explains why the death impulses of individual cells give rise (as they presumably do) to a death instinct of the organism as a whole. It is true that he presents a hypothesis concerning the mechanism through which the death impulses of individual cells are channeled in a multicellular organism to the destruction of external objects: this occurs through the muscular system (Freud 1923b, SE 19:41). But he does not address the more fundamental question of *why* the death instinct transfers itself from the cells to the multicellular organism as a whole.

If we overlook the problems of attributing a death instinct to individual cells and of explaining why the death instinct of cells transmits itself to the complex organism, and limit our considerations to the human organism as as whole, it may seem relatively easy to find instances of the death instinct. What could be more obvious than the fact that human beings engage in aggressive and destructive behavior? The problem here, however, is the assumption that aggressive and destructive impulses are in fact instances of the death instinct.

According to Freud, the death instinct is in essence an impulse to self-destruction, but becomes aggressive toward and destructive of others when it is diverted from the self. But it is not evident why the impulse of an organism to destroy itself by returning to its prior, inorganic state would "turn into" an impulse to destroy other beings (Freud 1933b [1932], SE 22:211). The desire to die seems quite different from the desire to inflict harm on external objects. How can the latter be a substitute for the former? Even Freud's loyal disciple Ernest Jones felt compelled to remark, "To pass from . . . a silent principle towards absolute peace . . . to the stormy aggressiveness that so disturbs mental life, is to pass from one world to quite another; and to identify the two opposites as one is a feat that few could genuinely encompass" (Jones 1936, p. 286).

According to the American Psychoanalytic Association's official *Glossary of Psychoanalytic Terms and Concepts*, the death instinct "has been severely criticized both within and without the psychoanalytic field. Most psychoanalysts assume that this formulation is a highly speculative one, which thus far cannot be confirmed by any biological investigation" (Moore and Fine 1968, p. 57). It is ironic that the new primal instinct that was to solve Freud's problem of where to locate aggressive impulses turns out to be itself so problematic.

In attempting to determine whether the death impulse meets the two criteria for an instinct, I shall deal only with the death instinct on the level of the human organism as a whole, and shall consider both its self-destructive and aggressive forms.

Does the death instinct involve tension caused by an endosomatic and constant stimulus? If in fact there is a death instinct in the human organism that somehow derives from the death impulses of its constituent cells, this instinct would clearly be endosomatic and constant. But would a stimulus be involved? If all organisms have an inherent tendency to self-destruction, it seems unnecessary to posit a stimulus to account for such a tendency. The existence of a stimulus is more plausible in the case of a human being's aggressive impulses; anger seems to be provoked by someone or something. But even if aggressive behavior does involve a tension-producing stimulus, there remains the problem of explaining how such behavior is a diverting of and substitute for an impulse to die.

The second criterion for an instinct is that there be pressure exerted on the mind to cause the organism to act to remove the tension created by the stimulus. Note that this criterion presupposes that the bearer of the instinct has a mind—a presupposition inconsistent with Freud's claim that the death instinct operates "in every particle of living substance" (Freud 1923b, SE 19:41). If having an instinct requires a mind, then substances without minds could not have a death instinct—or any instincts at all. This greatly expanded view of the domain of instincts in *Beyond the Pleasure Principle* is incompatible with the concept of instinct put forth in "Instincts and Their Vicissitudes" and elsewhere. But as noted earlier, Freud maintains his original view of the nature of instinct even after postulating his life-death classification theory in 1920.

My remarks here, however, are limited to the human organism, which does of course have a mind. When a person has in impulse to die, is pressure being exerted on the mind to act in a way that reduces tension caused by a stimulus? If one accepts Freud's thesis that the death wish is an inherent tendency, then there would seem to be no stimulus-caused tension in the first place. On a common sense level, of course, a person may wish to die as a means of escaping certain external stimuli. But for Freud, presumably, these external stimuli would simply trigger the internal instinct to die. (This would be analogous to the way external sexual stimuli trigger the internal sexual instinct; see Freud 1933a [1932], SE 22:96.) And the internal instinct to die would not seem to involve a stimulus.

With regard to human impulses to destroy external objects, the existence of stimuli that produce tension is plausible. So in these cases there may be "pressure" on a person's mind to cause him or her to act in a way that removes the tension. Even so, the problem remains: how are a person's aggressive impulses derivative of an impulse to die?

There are, then, serious difficulties in trying to fit the death instinct into Freud's general definition of instinct. Problems also arise when one applies the two criteria for instincts to the life instinct.

According to Freud, the life instinct, like the death instinct, permeates every level of every living being. It resides primarily in an organism's reproductive cells, but exists in all other cells as well, and is somehow transferred from the individual cells to the organism as a whole (see Freud 1920g, SE 18:52). The goal of the life instinct is to "form living substance into ever greater unities" (Freud 1923a [1922], SE 18:258) and, in the case of human beings, to effect "the unity of mankind" (Freud 1930a [1929], SE 21:122). In examining whether this impulse meets Freud's two criteria for an instinct, I shall (as when discussing the death instinct) limit my remarks to the instinct as it operates in the human organism as a whole.

The first condition that the life impulse must meet is that there be tension caused by an endosomatic and constant stimulus. If one grants that the life instinct in the human organism as a whole does arise from its cells, one could consider the instinct endosomatic and fairly constant. But what sort of endosomatic stimulus would cause a person to seek "ever greater unities"?

It is difficult to conceive of such an endo*somatic* stimulus, but Freud's doctrine of the life instinct as Eros hints that there might be an endo*psychic* stimulus. I refer to the "mythological" side of Freud's theory of Eros. When Freud speaks of Eros as a force that seeks the unity of all "living substance" (Freud 1920g, SE 18:60, n. 1; Freud 1923a [1922], SE 18:258), he seems to envision Eros as an entity in its own right, with its own plans for living creatures. From this perspective, Eros would be a cosmic force that influences the minds of human beings and guides civilization so as to achieve its goal of the unity of all life. This view of cosmic Eros is prominent in *Civilization and Its Discontents*, where Freud speaks of civilization as "a process in the service of Eros, whose purpose is to combine single human individuals, and after that families, then races, peoples and nations, into one great unity, the unity of mankind" (Freud 1930a [1929], SE 21:122).[5]

If cosmic Eros does instill in the individual an impulse for social union (see Freud 1930a [1929], SE 21:140), then there would be a stimulus involved in the life instinct. But since Eros would presumably implant its influence in the minds rather than the bodies of human beings, the life instinct still fails to meet the first criterion for an instinct; the stimulus would be endopsychic rather than endosomatic.

The second criterion the life impulse must meet if it is to qualify as an instinct is that there be pressure exerted on the mind to cause the organism to act in a way that reduces or eliminates the tension created by the stimulus. As I already observed when discussing the death instinct, this criterion assumes that the organism has a mind. So, strictly speaking, the life impulse does not fulfill this criterion because it operates not only in human beings, but in entities without minds, such as cells and (at the other end of the spectrum) families, races, and the human species as a whole. But even if we restrict ourselves to the life instinct as present in individual human beings, the second criterion is problematic: what kind of tension would be involved in the desire to live and to be united to other human beings?

Finally, since the life instinct includes all the sexual and ego impulses (except aggression) of Freud's early and middle periods, the difficulties raised in chapter 2 with regard to the definition of instinct apply to the life instinct as well. In short, the life instinct, like the death instinct, simply does not fit Freud's general concept of what an instinct is.

Prescinding from these difficulties, does Freud's life-death instinct classification theory mark an advance over his earlier sexual-ego schema? Freud considers his new theory superior because it enables him to posit an essential unity of the sexual and ego impulses (the problematic implication of his analysis of narcissism), and yet maintain an instinctual dualism: in the new schema the sexual and ego impulses are two manifestations of a primal life instinct, united in battle against an equally primal death instinct. This may be a theoretical advance, but if so, it is purchased at considerable cost. For in introducing his theory of the life and death instincts, Freud not only goes well beyond his general concept of instinct, but also leaves the more empirical ground of clinical and everyday observation for the more imaginative realm of cosmic speculation. The conflict in the neurotic's mind between sexual desires and personal or social ideals has given way to a cosmic battle constantly being fought in every particle of living substance between the forces of Life and Death.

Despite the widespread opposition his life-death theory encountered, Freud became increasingly convinced of the truth of his new theory. Nine years after first postulating the death instinct in *Beyond the Pleasure Principle*, he wrote:

> The assumption of the existence of an instinct of death or destruction has met with resistance even in analytic circles . . . To begin with it was only tentatively that I put forward [these] views, but in the course of time they have gained such a hold on me that I can no longer think in any other way. (Freud 1930a [1929], SE 21:119)

With this discussion of the final stage of Freud's views on the classification of instincts, we come to the end of Part One. Now that we have analyzed Freud's theory of instincts — both his general notion of instincts and his three attempts to categorize the instincts — we are in a position to see what moral philosophy is implicit in that theory.

Freud's Moral Philosophy

Freud's Implicit
Moral Theory

FREUD would strongly reject the suggestion that psychoanalysis contains a moral theory. According to Freud, psychoanalysis is a science, and as such is concerned only with facts, not with values. But if a moral theory is a set of guidelines for the living of one's life, and if one should live one's life in a way that fulfills one's nature, then psychoanalysis does contain a moral theory. For psychoanalysis presents a comprehensive view of what human nature is, and its implicit moral directive would be that a person should act in a way that fulfills his or her nature, psychoanalytically understood. That a moral theory is a set of guidelines for living seems true by definition. That one should live in a way that fulfills one's nature is a philosophical assumption basic to my argument in this book.

As I pointed out in the Introduction, although Freud himself never says explicitly that human beings should fulfill their nature, his approach to psychotherapy indicates that he does accept this view. The aim of psychoanalytic therapy is to cure neurotic patients by helping them understand their human nature and enabling them to live in a way consonant with it. In those cases in which the analyst plays the role of teacher and mentor, "the patient should be educated to liberate and fulfil his own nature, not to resemble [the analyst]" (Freud 1919a [1918], SE 17:165). An analyst who encourages patients to live in a manner beyond the capacity of their human nature is likely to induce renewed neurotic suffering (Freud 1912e, SE 12:118–119). And since we are all neurotic in some ways ("We are all to some extent hysterics" [Freud 1905d, SE 7:171]), the therapeutic goal of understanding our nature and living according to this knowledge presumably holds for everyone, not just for people undergoing therapy.

What is this human nature that we should all try to fulfill? It consists fundamentally of instincts: "The deepest essence of human nature consists in instinctual impulses which are of an elementary nature, which are similar in all men and which aim at the satisfaction of certain primal needs" (Freud 1915b, SE 14:281). So the way to become psychologically healthier and live happier lives is to learn to satisfy our instincts more effectively. The Freudian moral imperative, that is to say, is that we should satisfy our instincts as fully as we can.

My claim that according to psychoanalytic theory we fulfill our nature by fulfilling our instincts might be challenged on the grounds that our nature consists of more than the id, which is "the repository of the instinctual impulses" (Freud 1926f [1925], SE 20:266). Since we not only have an id (*das Es*, literally "the it"), but also an ego and a superego, one might argue that we should satisfy the demands of one or both of these other psychic agencies rather than those of the id. But the ego and the superego grow out of the id (p. 266; Freud 1933a [1932], SE 22:76–77), and, like the id, are subject to the pleasure principle (Freud 1916–17 [1915–17], SE 16:356–357; Freud 1920g, SE 18:7). When the ego tries to mediate the demands of the id for immediate pleasure, the realities of the external world, and the ideals of the superego (Freud 1923b, SE 19:56; Freud 1933a [1932] SE 22:77–78), it does so on the basis of what will ultimately cause the most pleasure or the least unpleasure. The business of the ego, Freud explains, "is to discover the most favourable and least perilous method of obtaining [instinctual] satisfaction" (Freud 1940a [1938], SE 23:148).

Freud's theory of the psyche is essentially reductionistic, and since the id is "the core of our being" (Freud 1940a [1938], SE 23:197), we fulfill our nature by following the pleasure principle, which "reigns unrestrictedly [i.e., without being modified by the reality principle] in the id" (Freud 1923b, SE 19:25). As Freud remarks in *An Outline of Psycho-Analysis*, the id is the "oldest portion of the psychical apparatus [and] the most important throughout life" (Freud 1940a [1938], SE 23:145, n. 2). By following the pleasure principle and satisfying the id's instincts we achieve our purpose in life: "The power of the id expresses the true purpose of the individual organism's life. This consists in the satisfaction of its innate needs" (p. 148).

By itself, the directive to satisfy one's instincts is too general to be an informative moral theory; we would need to know more about which impulses qualify as instincts. But Freud, as we have seen in Part One, has a good deal to say about the nature and classification of instincts, and his detailed views on human instincts lead to a fairly comprehensive moral theory. The present chapter argues that the moral philosophy implicit in Freud's theory of instincts can be best characterized as individualistic hedonism. The following chapter discusses the compatibility of Freud's moral individualism with his explanations of the dynamics of group psychology.

The task of delineating what it would mean, on the basis of Freud's theory of instincts, for a person to satisfy his or her instinctual impulses is complicated by the fact that Freud does not have just one theory about instincts. He has a general concept of what an instinct is (chapter 1); a theory of sexual-ego dualism, in which neither the sexual nor the ego instinct completely fits the general concept of instinct (chapter 2); a theory that continues to claim the irreducibility of the sexual and ego instincts, despite the acknowledged difficulty of maintaining this view (chapter 3); and a theory of a life-death dualism, in which neither of these impulses meets the general criteria for an instinct (chapter 4).

These various Freudian theories about instincts yield three different approaches to answering the question of how life is to be lived. The first approach is based on the definition of instinct: once one knows what an instinct is, one can try to determine which impulses are instinctual and how best to satisfy them. The second way is to assume with Freud, in his early and middle periods, that the two primordial instincts are the sexual and ego impulses (overlooking the problems of fitting these impulses into Freud's general concept of instinct), and then determine what different forms these impulses take and how best to satisfy these impulses in their various forms. Third, one can accept Freud's late instinct classification theory and try to live one's life in a way that satisfies the life and the death instincts (once again prescinding from the fact that neither type of impulse actually fits the definition of instinct).

Each approach yields a somewhat different moral theory. I shall argue that the first leads to a rather general yet identifiable moral theory: individualistic hedonism. The second approach also implies an individualistic hedonism, but this time the theory takes on more detail, since Freud specifies the sexual and ego impulses as the basic instincts and (as we shall see) discusses various indirect methods of satisfying sexual impulses. The third way yields no definite moral theory, for it is not clear how one should go about satisfying the death instinct—and even less clear how one could satisfy this instinct and the life instinct at the same time.

The first approach is based simply on Freud's concept of instinct as something that exerts pressure on the mind to cause an organism to act in a way that eliminates or reduces the tension caused by endosomatic and fairly constant stimuli. If a person is to fulfill his or her nature, and if that nature consists essentially of instincts, then he or she should live in a way that effectively reduces instinctual tension. To reduce tension causes pleasure, and cause and effect are so closely related here that Freud at times identifies them (e.g., Freud 1920g, SE 18:7). If one grants this identity, the moral precept implied by Freud's definition of instinct is that a person should try to experience pleasure. It seems fair to infer that, according to this doctrine, a person should not strive simply for pleasure, but for as much pleasure as possible.

This moral doctrine is both a hedonism and an individualism. It is a hedonism because (1) it claims that only pleasure (*hēdonē*) is intrinsically good; anything else has value only insofar as it produces pleasure; (2) it claims that all pleasure is intrinsically good; all reduction of tension is good, regardless of the nature of the tension or the nature of the means by which the tension is reduced; (3) it claims that pleasures differ only in quantity; one pleasure can be considered better than another only because it removes more tension, not because of any qualitative difference between the two pleasures. Note that hedonism here does not necessarily imply libertinism; direct satisfaction of an instinct can, in the long run, create more tension than it removes. In Freud's terminology, the pleasure principle must include its corollary, the reality principle (Freud 1920g, SE 18:10–11).

Some scholars deny that Freud's theory is hedonistic. In *Freud: The Mind of the Moralist*, Philip Rieff argues that because Freud understood pleasure as simply a transition from an excess to a deficiency of tension, he could not have held pleasure to be the goal of life: "Far from advancing the ethical hedonism with which he is mistakenly charged, Freud in his psychology of pleasure indicates the futility of hedonism . . . . The Freudian psychology reveals the ephemeral quality of pleasure as an end in itself" (Rieff 1979 [first ed. 1959], pp. 326–327). However, although Freud does hold that pleasure (tension reduction) is ephemeral, it is nevertheless for him the goal of every psychic process (Freud 1920g, SE 18:7); the pleasure resulting from the satisfaction of instincts is "the true purpose of the individual organism's life" (Freud 1940a [1938], SE 23:148).

According to Rieff, Freud does not counsel us to follow the pleasure principle. Rather, "it is toward the reality principle that Freud turns us, toward the sober business of living" (Rieff 1979, p. 324). But in drawing an opposition between the pleasure principle and the reality principle, Rieff overlooks the fact that the latter is simply an extension of the former. The reason for adopting the reality principle is that it is a more effective way of carrying out the program of the pleasure principle; we can get more pleasure in the admittedly "sober business of living" if we take reality into account when choosing what to do. Freud states that the reality principle, like the pleasure principle, "at bottom seeks to obtain pleasure" (Freud 1916–17 [1915–17], SE 16:357). As Freud remarks in a letter to Ernest Jones, "The reality principle is only continuing the work of the pleasure principle in a more effectual way, gratification being the aim of both" (letter of January 14, 1912, quoted in Jones 1955, p. 453).

James Daley also denies that Freud's theory is hedonistic. "It is not hedonism in the traditional sense that pleasure and pleasure only is good and the sole aim of human behavior" (Daley 1967–68, p. 208). According to Daley, Freud's endorsement of the constancy principle shows that he views harmony (and not pleasure alone) as intrinsically good (pp. 203–205). But this is to misunderstand the constancy principle. According to Freud, we try to keep our "quantity of excitation . . . as low as possible or at least to keep it constant" precisely because "anything that is calculated to increase that quantity is bound to be felt as . . . unpleasurable" (Freud 1920g, SE 18:9). That is to say, the "harmony" (not Freud's term) sought by the constancy principle is not valuable in itself, but only as a means of avoiding unpleasure.[1]

The moral doctrine flowing from Freud's concept of instinct is not only a hedonism, but an individualism: it claims that one should seek one's own individual pleasure, rather than that of other people, or of other people and oneself. The effects of one's actions on other people should be taken into account only insofar as they affect one's own experience of pleasure. For example, a person who gets pleasure from helping others may be advised to do so, but the ultimate rationale would be that such activity brings pleasure to the agent.[2]

The doctrine of individualistic hedonism implicit in Freud's general definition of instinct provides a moral rule for action that is broad enough to cover most situations: do that which maximizes your own pleasure. The only situations not covered are those in which two or more alternatives would each yield the same amount of pleasure; in such cases each alternative would be equally moral. This moral theory, however, says nothing about what types of instincts there are, or about the various direct and indirect ways in which we can reduce instinctual tension and thereby attain pleasure.

The moral theory implied by the sexual-ego instinct classification theory of Freud's early and middle periods is also an individualistic hedonism, but this version is considerably more concrete. Because this instinct theory categorizes the various human impulses and explains the different forms they take, it offers more specific guidance on how to reduce tension and thus experience pleasure.

Freud's sexual-ego theory would not seem, at first glance, to lead to hedonism. Freud contrasts the sexual instincts with the ego instincts, and the contrast seems to be precisely between those instincts that aim at pleasure (the sexual instincts) and those that aim at something other than pleasure (the ego instincts). The Freudian directive here is not just to fulfill one's sexual impulses (which would of course be a hedonism), but to fulfill one's sexual *and* ego impulses. And since the ego impulses can often oppose the pleasure-oriented sexual impulses, the moral theory here would seem to be something other than hedonism. The theory would still be an individualism, since one is to satisfy one's own sexual and ego impulses, not those of other people. But it would not be an individualistic *hedonism*, since the satisfaction of one's own ego instincts would rank alongside pleasure as an intrinsic good.

Do the ego instincts, however, really aim at something other than pleasure? Freud defines the ego instincts without making reference to pleasure: they are those impulses aiming at "self-preservation," i.e., at the continuance of one's physical existence, the enhancement of one's life, and the maintenance of one's idealized self-image. But it seems legitimate to ask, in the context of psychoanalytic theory, *why* an organism tries to preserve itself.

Freud's hypothesis of the pleasure principle suggests that an organism seeks to preserve itself as a means of attaining pleasure. According to Freud, "the course taken by mental events is automatically regulated by the pleasure principle" (Freud 1920g, SE

18:7). That is to say, every mental operation is governed by the aim of reducing tension and thereby eliminating unpleasure and producing pleasure. Since the ego instincts are mental operations, they must have the ultimate goal of causing pleasure for the organism. So while one can agree with Freud that the ego instincts aim at self-preservation, self-preservation is itself subordinate to the goal of producing pleasure.

Freud's analysis of repression supports my view that the ego instincts, in Freud's early and middle classification theories, are subject to the pleasure principle. Repression occurs when the ego refuses to admit certain sexual desires to consciousness because they conflict with a person's self-image. In other words, the ego instincts repress sexual instincts because the failure to do so would lead to unpleasure: "The motive and purpose of repression [is] nothing else than the avoidance of unpleasure" (Freud 1915d, SE 14:153; see Freud 1920g, SE 18:11). So this activity of the ego instincts is in fact ruled by the pleasure principle. (And when repression creates a neurotic symptom, the symptom itself is "in its essence a substitutive sexual satisfaction," i.e., a substitutive pleasure [Freud 1923a (1922), SE 18:246].)

Because both the ego instincts and the sexual instincts aim at pleasure, the ethical theory implied by Freud's sexual-ego classification schema is a hedonism. And because a person is to seek his or her own individual pleasure, the theory is one of individualistic hedonism.

The fact that all impulses aim at pleasure enables psychoanalysis to provide a rule for deciding what to do when one has incompatible wishes: satisfy the impulse that will yield the most pleasure. The pleasure principle, in other words, should be the basis for settling conflicts between impulses—whether the conflict is between impulses in the same category (sexual or ego) or between impulses in different categories.

There is a paradox, however, in saying that the pleasure principle *should* be used to resolve conflicts; for as stated by Freud the pleasure principle is something that actually *does* govern human action (see Abramson 1984, pp. 114–119). If a person's actions are in fact already determined by the goal of maximizing pleasure (the doctrine called "psychological hedonism"), what is the point of laying down the moral precept that a person should maximize pleasure ("ethical hedonism")?

Freud himself does not address this paradox. It would be surprising if he did, for while he expressly holds psychological hedonism, he denies that psychoanalysis contains any ethical theory, hedonistic or nonhedonistic. Nonetheless, I think that one can formulate a Freudian explanation of the relationship between psychoanalysis's explicit psychological hedonism and its implicit doctrine of ethical hedonism. The explanation is based on Freud's view that the goal of psychotherapy is to strengthen the self (ego).

According to Freud, "The poor ego . . . serves three severe masters and does what it can to bring their claims and demands into harmony with one another . . . . Its three tyrannical masters are the external world, the super-ego and the id" (Freud 1933a [1932] SE 22:77). The goal of therapy is to help the ego meet the demands of these masters more effectively; therapy tries "to strengthen the ego, to make it more independent of the super-ego, to widen its field of perception [i.e., perception of external reality] and enlarge its organization, so that it can appropriate fresh portions of the id. Where id was, there ego shall be" (p. 80).

Freud's remarks on ego strength suggest that both a weak and a strong ego do in fact act in accordance with the pleasure principle (psychological hedonism), but that a weak ego is less successful in the pursuit of pleasure. Someone with a weak ego, therefore, *should* seek pleasure (ethical hedonism), in the sense of trying to be more effective in his or her efforts. To be more effective will require making more intelligent and better informed judgments about what actions will yield pleasure, and this in turn will require dealing more rationally with the superego, the id, and external reality. And since every ego, however weak or strong, presumably can be strengthened further, the moral precept to seek pleasure more effectively applies to everyone.

This line of thought seems to be a properly Freudian response to the problem of reconciling psychological and ethical hedonism, but it is not wholly satisfying. Since all mental events are ruled by the pleasure principle, the decision whether or not to pursue pleasure more effectively will *itself* be made on the basis of pleasure. And surely it is paradoxical to say that someone should pursue pleasure more effectively if his or her response to this moral demand is already determined by the pleasure principle. The problem comes down to that of freedom and determinism: the Freudian directive to maximize pleasure seems to presuppose that human beings are free to choose whether or not to seek this goal, while the pleasure principle implies that every human action is in fact determined by the goal of maximizing pleasure. Freud does not seem to appreciate the tension in psychoanalytic theory between freedom and determinism.

Be that as it may, the individualistic hedonism implied by Freud's sexual-ego classification theory is more specific than the individualistic hedonism implied by his general definition of instinct. First, it specifies sexual and ego impulses as the basic human impulses, and thus provides a framework for sorting out one's many and varied desires. Second, it offers some guidance in situations where one has to decide which of two or more incompatible sexual impulses to satisfy. Such rules for choice can be inferred from Freud's theories about how sexual desires are transformed through various psychic mechanisms into seemingly nonsexual desires.

It will be helpful to take a look at some of these psychic mechanisms. I shall discuss three of them: aim inhibition, sublimation, and reaction formation.

Freud describes an instinct as "inhibited in its aim" when it is "allowed to make some advance toward instinctual satisfaction but [is] then inhibited or deflected" (Freud 1915c, SE 14:122). This description is intended to apply to all instincts, but every example that Freud gives of aim inhibition seems to be of a sexual instinct. Specifically sexual aim-inhibited instincts are defined as those impulses that "have not abandoned their directly sexual aims, but are held back by certain internal resistances from attaining them; they rest content with certain approximations to satisfaction" (Freud 1923a [1922], SE 18:258).

In this context, "directly sexual" aims seem to refer to genital activity; in one work Freud equates "fully sensual love" with "genital love," and contrasts this kind of love with aim-inhibited love (Freud 1930a [1929], SE 21:102–103). However, according to Freud children as well as adults engage in sexual activity, and since the mechanism of aim inhibition is said to be operative in children, "directly sexual" must include nongenital activities. In fact, the best way to understand the notion of aim inhibition is to analyze the phenomenon as it occurs in children.

When a child moves beyond its initial state of primary narcissism, it directs its libido toward its parent (or parent-substitute) of the opposite sex as its first object. The child wants to possess that parent. The child's other parent, however, is perceived as a rival, and the child therefore wishes that this other parent would disappear or die. This set of feelings toward its parents constitutes the well-known Oedipus complex (see Freud 1900a [1899], SE 4:260–264). For a variety of reasons, e.g., a boy's fear that his father will punish him by castration (see Freud 1924d, SE 19:173–179), the child represses his or her sensual desires for the parent of the opposite sex. After such repression "the child still remains tied to his parents, but by instincts which must be described as being 'inhibited in their aim'" (Freud 1921c, SE 18:111). The child's sensual desires for the parent of the opposite sex are replaced with "a purely affectionate emotional tie . . . , no longer to be described as 'sexual'" (p. 138).

According to Freud, every feeling of affection in later life that does not aim at sensual gratification is, similarly, a transformation of an originally sexual desire:

> Wherever we come across an affectionate feeling it is successor to a completely 'sensual' object-tie . . . . We are justified in saying that [affectionate ties] have been diverted from [their] sexual aims . . . . Moreover, those instincts which are inhibited in their aims always preserve some few of their original sexual aims; even as an affectionate devotee, even a

friend or an admirer, desires the physical proximity and sight of the person. (pp. 138–139)

Included among the aim-inhibited instincts are "the affectionate relations between parents and children . . . , feelings of friendship, and the emotional ties in marriage" (Freud 1923a [1922], SE 18:258). In addition, every feeling of tenderness "undoubtedly originates from the sources of sexual need and invariably renounces its satisfaction" (Freud 1933a [1932], SE 22:97). Sexual desires can also be diverted to nonpersonal objects, e.g., to a love of beauty. Freud remarks in *Civilization and Its Discontents* that "all that seems certain [about beauty] is its derivation from the field of sexual feeling. The love of beauty seems a perfect example of an impulse inhibited in its aim. 'Beauty' and 'attraction' are originally attributes of the sexual object" (Freud 1930a [1929], SE 21:83). According to Freud, the original meaning of "beautiful" was "sexually stimulating" (Freud 1905d [1915 add.], SE 7:156, n. 2; Freud 1905d, SE 7:209).

Freud claims that an aim-inhibited sexual instinct does not lead to full instinctual satisfaction: the original sexual instinct makes "some advance" towards satisfaction, but attains only "a partial satisfaction" (Freud 1915c, SE 14:122). So the pleasure derived from such activities as friendship and aesthetic appreciation is incomplete because these activities are only substitutes for what is more fundamentally desired, namely, sexual activity. And the substitute is no match for the real thing.

There is a problem with Freud's theory of aim inhibition, however. According to Freud an aim-inhibited instinct is "no longer to be described as 'sexual'" (Freud 1921c, SE 18:138), is not "directly sexual" (Freud 1923a [1922], SE 18:258). Yet an aim-inhibited instinct still aims at pleasure. If, as I have argued, all instincts that aim at pleasure are by definition sexual, then an aim-inhibited instinct is just as directly sexual as an uninhibited instinct. The fact that an impulse is diverted from a *genital* aim does not mean that it is diverted from a *sexual* aim, for (as Freud himself emphasizes), "sexual" has a wider meaning than "genital".

There is a way to circumvent this difficulty and still preserve the main point of Freud's theory of aim inhibition: one could say that an uninhibited sexual instinct aims at full (rather than "directly sexual") satisfaction, whereas an aim-inhibited instinct aims at partial (rather than "nonsexual") satisfaction.

The theory of aim inhibition has implications for Freud's moral philosophy of individualistic hedonism. All things being equal, a person trying to maximize his or her own pleasure should fulfill uninhibited sexual instincts rather than inhibited ones, since this will yield greater pleasure. In many situations, of course, all things are not equal. For example, an attempt to satisfy certain uninhibited sexual impulses may lead to punitive action by one's superego, unpleasurable social consequences, or both. In such cases one must judge whether the prospective unpleasure will outweigh the prospective pleasure. That is to say, in following the pleasure principle one must take into consideration the reality principle. Nonetheless, the general ethical principle stands: full satisfaction is preferable to partial satisfaction.

A word is in order here about the role of the superego in morality. Since the superego is, in a certain sense, the voice of morality, it may seem paradoxical to list punitive action by one's superego as just one of several factors to be considered when deciding whether to fulfill an inhibited or an uninhibited sexual impulse. How could it ever be moral to go against the demands of one's superego in any context at all?

The answer lies in understanding in what sense, for Freud, the superego is the "voice of morality." According to Freud, the superego is formed when a child "identifies" with its parents, taking their ideals and moral standards into its own ego. The superego is thus "the representative of our relation to our parents. When we were little children we knew these higher natures, we admired them and feared them; and later we took them into ourselves" (Freud 1923b, SE 19:36; see Freud 1933a [1932], SE 22:63–64). And as we grow older, the role of our parents "is carried on by teachers and others in authority; their injunctions and prohibitions remain powerful in the ego ideal [superego] and continue . . . to exercise the moral censorship" (Freud 1923b, SE 19:37; see Freud 1940a

[1938], SE 23:146). The superego becomes distinct from the ego, standing above it (hence the term *Über-Ich*, "above-I") and presenting it with "the ethical standards of mankind" (Freud 1925d [1924], SE 20:59). The superego praises the ego when it follows these standards and reproaches it when it falls short.

The superego is the voice of morality, then, in the sense of being the internalization of the ideals of one's parents and of one's culture. So when Freud says that it is only by the formation of the superego that a child "become[s] a moral and social being" (Freud 1927c, SE 21:11), he means "moral" in the sense of adhering to society's standards of conduct. But to be moral in this sense is not necessarily the same as being moral in the sense employed in this book. As I have stated previously, by acting morally I mean doing what fulfills one's human nature. And according to Freud's implicit moral philosophy, to fulfill one's human nature means to maximize one's pleasure. Cultural norms for action may not (and according to Freud often do not) promote one's own pleasure. So for an individualistic hedonist, the pleasure or pain resulting from following or violating the dictates of the superego is just one of several factors to be considered when deciding how to act. If the pleasures resulting from an action contravening the demands of the superego outweigh the pains, then an individualistic hedonist *should* violate his or her superego; to follow the "voice of morality" in such a case would be *im*moral.

The second psychic mechanism a person can use to create a substitute satisfaction for a sexual instinct is sublimation. Freud's first published use of the term "sublimate" occurs in his *Three Essays on the Theory of Sexuality*, in a discussion of sexual stimulation through looking:

> Visual impressions remain the most frequent pathway along which libidinal excitation is aroused . . . . The progressive concealment of the body which goes along with civilization keeps sexual curiosity awake. This curiosity seeks to complete the sexual object by revealing its hidden parts. It can, however, be diverted ('sublimated') in the direction of art, if its

interest can be shifted away from the genitals on to the shape of the body as a whole. (Freud 1905d, SE 7:156)

Not every diversion of a sexual instinct is a sublimation; the diverting must be to an aim that is "other than sexual" (p. 206), though "psychically related" to the original sexual aim (Freud 1908d, SE 9:187). This new "desexualized" aim (Freud 1923b, SE 19:45), moreover, must be "higher" than the original one, i.e., "socially valuable" (Freud 1910a [1909], SE 11:54). That is to say, the diverting of a sexual impulse counts as sublimation only if the new activity benefits society. Sublimation, in short, "consists in the sexual trend abandoning its aim of obtaining a component or a reproductive pleasure and taking on another which is related genetically to the abandoned one but is itself no longer sexual and must be described as social" (Freud 1916–17 [1915–17], SE 16:345).

Freud's chief example of sublimation is art. According to Freud, the production of works of art is a sublimation of the sexual instinct of exhibitionism (the desire to display one's genitals) (Freud 1905d, SE 7:157, 166–169, 192). The desire to be an actor or actress is likewise a sublimation of exhibitionism (Freud 1910a [1909], SE 11:44). Another instance of sublimation is "the instinct for knowledge or research," which is a transformation of scopophilia (the desire to look at other people's genitals) and of a desire for mastery (Freud 1905d [1915 add.], SE 7:194). Scientific inquiry is thus a sublimated sexual activity (Freud 1930a [1929], SE 21:97); indeed, Freud sees science as "the most complete renunciation of the pleasure principle of which our mental activity is capable" (Freud 1910h, SE 11:165). Artistic and scientific activities are "higher" than impulses to exhibitionism, scopophilia, and mastery because they benefit society.

There is a theoretical problem with Freud's theory of sublimation, similar to the problem I raised when discussing aim inhibition. Freud holds that in the process of sublimation, a sexual aim is replaced with one that is "other than sexual" (Freud 1905d, SE 7:206), "asexual" (Freud 1905e, SE 7:50), "no longer sexual"

(Freud 1908d, SE 9:187), "desexualized" (Freud 1923b, SE 19:45), etc. Nevertheless, the new aim, like the former one, is a form of pleasure (Freud 1916–17 [1915–17], SE 16:345). But since every impulse that aims at pleasure is by definition sexual, a sublimated impulse is just as sexual as a nonsublimated one. So the difference between sublimated and nonsublimated impulses is not one between sexual and nonsexual aims, but rather between genital (or closely allied) aims and nongenital ones.

What are the implications of the psychic mechanism of sublimation for the intelligent pursuit of pleasure? A sublimated activity is, for Freud, merely a substitute for the originally intended, nonsublimated activity. And since the original activity is presumably more pleasurable than a substitute, it is (all things being equal) preferable to it. At any rate, one must take into account one's individual capacity for sublimation; not everyone can sublimate instinctual urges with the same ease or to the same extent. In this context, Freud cautions analysts about encouraging patients to sublimate desires that are no longer repressed: "Not every neurotic has a high talent for sublimation . . . . If we press them unduly towards sublimation and cut them off from the most accessible and convenient instinctual satisfactions, we shall usually make life even harder for them" (Freud 1912e, SE 12:119).

In deciding whether or not to sublimate an impulse, should we take into account the fact that a sublimated activity is socially desirable, whereas a nonsublimated one is not? Would this be a valid moral reason for choosing sublimation? Not on the basis of Freud's moral theory of individualistic hedonism. For according to that theory, a person should try to maximize his or her own pleasure, not that of other members of society. Of course, if giving pleasure to others increases our own pleasure (e.g., from the approval of our superego) or prevents our own unpleasure (e.g., from chastisement by our superego), then we have reason to choose a sublimated activity. But all in all, nonsublimated pleasures are to be preferred.

A third way in which sexual instincts are transformed is through "reaction formation."[3] Freud introduces this notion in his discussion of infantile sexuality in the *Three Essays*. A child has sexual desires, and comes to realize that society disapproves of this. In order to avoid the unpleasure of disapproval, the child builds up certain mental forces that

> impede the course of the sexual instinct and, like dams, restrict its flow—[namely,] disgust, feelings of shame and the claims of aesthetic and moral ideals . . . . The sexual impulses . . . evoke opposing mental forces (reacting impulses) which, in order to suppress . . . unpleasure effectively, build up . . . mental dams. (Freud 1905d, SE 7:177–178)

In his *Introductory Lectures* Freud describes reaction formations as "the anticathexes opposing the demands of the instincts" (Freud 1916–17 [1915–17], SE 16:375). An anticathexis is an investment of energy made by the ego to defend itself against the threat of a cathexis that has already been established (Freud 1925d [1924], SE 20:30; see Freud 1915c, SE 14:181). The cathexes in question are those seeking instinctual satisfaction—more specifically, satisfaction of the sexual instincts. Reaction formations, in short, are "assurances against sexual satisfaction" (Freud 1923a [1922], SE 18:247).

Freud analyzes a child's demand that everyone be treated equally as a reaction formation against feelings of envy toward those children who receive special treatment. The child reasons, "If one cannot be the favourite oneself, at all events nobody else shall be the favourite" (Freud 1921c, SE 18:120).

Desires of adults for social justice derive from this early childhood reaction formation:

> Social justice means that we deny ourselves many things so that others may have to do without them as well, or, what is the same thing, may not be able to ask for them. This demand for equality is at the root of social conscience and the sense of duty . . . . Thus social feeling is based upon the reversal of what was at first a hostile feeling into a postively-toned tie. (p. 121)

Altruism is a reaction formation against selfishness, and pity a reaction formation against cruelty (Freud 1915b, SE 14:281). According to Freud, "Social feelings arise in the individual as a superstructure built upon impulses of jealous rivalry against his brothers and sisters" (Freud 1923b, SE 19:37). Furthermore, "Conscience is itself a reaction-formation against the evil that is perceived in the id" (Freud 1925i, SE 19:134).

In some instances, a reaction formation is simply the intensification of a feeling that was already present to some degree, rather than the creation of a completely new feeling. Freud observes that people often have conflicting feelings toward the same object. One way the psyche has of dealing with this ambivalence is to exaggerate one feeling (e.g., love) and repress the opposing one (e.g., hate):

> One of the two conflicting feelings (usually that of affection) becomes enormously intensified and the other vanishes. The exaggerated degree and compulsive character of the affection alone betray the fact that it is not the only one present but is continually on the alert to keep the opposite feeling under suppression, and enables us to postulate the operation of a process which we call repression by means of *reaction-formation*. (Freud 1926d [1925], SE 20:102, Freud's emphasis; see pp. 157–158)

Freud's concept of reaction formation raises a problem similar to those raised by aim inhibition and sublimation. Freud says that reaction formations oppose "the course of the sexual instinct" (Freud 1905d, SE 7:177), and are "assurances against sexual satisfaction" (Freud 1923a [1922], SE 18:247). But according to Freud a reaction formation still aims at pleasure, for it arises "in order to suppress . . . unpleasure" (Freud 1905d, SE 7:178), and for Freud, the elimination of unpleasure is synonymous with the production of pleasure. Since all pleasure-seeking impulses are by definition sexual, the process of reaction formation does not really prevent sexual satisfaction; it simply replaces one type of sexual satisfaction with another.

Would a person trying to follow the moral philosophy of individualistic hedonism be better advised to carry out a sexual impulse in its original form, or to satisfy an impulse arising in reaction against it? Everything else being equal, it would seem preferable to follow the original impulse, since satisfying this desire would presumably bring more pleasure than satisfying a merely derivative —and antithetical—substitute. Moreover, by satisfying the initial desire one would avoid expending psychic energy to maintain the repression involved in reaction formation; this energy could be more profitably spent on a more direct pursuit of pleasure. It will rarely happen, however, that in a given situation all other things are, in fact, equal. The pleasure of gratifying one's original desire may be outweighed by the unpleasure that could result from the disapproval of other people, of one's superego, etc. The reality principle, in other words, may dictate that one follow the path of reaction formation. Freud seems to have such situations in mind when he remarks that the mechanism of reaction formation, which begins in childhood, "continues in favourable cases throughout [one's] whole life" (p. 238).

Once a person has become aware that certain desires he or she has are not original impulses, but merely substitutes produced through such processes as aim inhibition, sublimation, and reaction formation, he or she can begin to consider whether more pleasure would result from satisfying the substitute desire. The decision of which desire to follow will depend largely upon the consequences an action would bring from other members of society. Social approval of one's action will cause a certain amount of pleasure, and social disapproval—not to mention sanctions—will cause unpleasure. But it is important to keep in mind that according to the theory of individualistic hedonism, the positive or negative effect that one's actions have on other people is in itself not morally relevant; the only thing that ultimately matters is the effect on oneself. For example, the "socially valuable" aspect of a sublimated activity is not in itself a reason for choosing this activity over the nonsublimated alternative; the social consequences are relevant only insofar as they affect the individual concerned.

Society as such, of course, cannot endorse an ethical theory of individualistic hedonism. If society were to allow individuals to seek unrestrictedly the satisfaction of their instincts, it would sign its own death warrant. Human beings would end up returning to their primeval state—which was, in Freud's view, a brutal and unsocial one:

> [Primeval man] had no objection to someone else's death; it meant the annihilation of someone he hated, and primitive man had no scruples against bringing it about. He was no doubt a very passionate creature and more cruel and more malignant than other animals. He liked to kill, and killed as a matter of course. The instinct which is said to restrain other animals from killing and devouring their own species need not be attributed to him. (Freud 1915b, SE 14:292)

Freud describes the fundamental realtionship of one human being to another as *homo homini lupus*, "Man is a wolf to man":[4]

> Men are not gentle creatures who want to be loved, and who at the most can defend themselves if they are attacked; they are, on the contrary, creatures among whose instinctual endowments is to be reckoned a powerful share of aggressiveness. As a result, their neighbor is for them not only a potential helper or sexual object, but also someone who tempts them to satisfy their aggressiveness on him, to exploit his capacity for work without compensation, to use him sexually without his consent, to seize his possessions, to humiliate him, to cause him pain, to torture and to kill him. *Homo homini lupus.* (Freud 1930a [1929], SE 21:111)

Human beings developed civilization in order to protect themselves against the aggression of other people (p. 95) and against the harshness of nature (Freud 1927c, SE 21:15). While civilization does provide individuals with this twofold protection, it exacts a heavy price: the renunciation of many of their instinctual aims.

According to Freud, there is a fundamental conflict between the individual and society—a theme he discusses in a number of his writings. In 1908 he states that "civilization is built up on the suppression of instincts" (Freud 1908d, SE 9:186). Four years later he makes the "gloomy prognosis" that since it seems "quite impossible to adjust the claims of the sexual instinct to the demands of civilization," in the process of cultural development "renunciation and suffering . . . cannot be avoided by the human race" (Freud 1912d, SE 11:190).

In his *Introductory Lectures* Freud emphasizes the threat sexual instincts pose to society:

> We believe that civilization has been created under the pressure of the exigencies of life at the cost of satisfaction of the instincts; and we believe that . . . each individual who makes fresh entry into human society repeats this sacrifice . . . for the benefit of the whole community. Among the instinctual forces which are put to this use the sexual impulses play an important part . . . . Society believes that no greater threat to its civilization could arise than if the sexual instincts were to be liberated and returned to their original aims. (Freud 1916–17 [1915–17], SE 15:22–23)

Freud declares in 1927 that "every individual is virtually an enemy of civilization, though civilization is supposed to be an object of universal human interest" (Freud 1927c, SE 21:6). In *Civilization and Its Discontents* he explains that when society begins to form, "the members of the community restrict themselves in their possibilities of satisfaction, whereas the individual [previously] knew no such restrictions," and remarks that "it is impossible to overlook the extent to which civilization is built up upon a renunciation of instinct" (Freud 1930a [1929], SE 21:95, 97).

In a work written three years later Freud makes it clear that society requires individuals to renounce not only their sexual impulses, but their aggressive impulses as well:

> It has become our habit to say that our civilization has been built up at the cost of sexual trends . . . . What we have come to see about the sexual instincts, applies equally and perhaps still more to the other ones, the aggressive instincts. It is they above all that make human communal life difficult and threaten its survival. (Freud 1933a [1932], SE 22:110)

Is the conflict between the individual and society irreconcilable, or might there be some form of civilization that can accommodate the needs of both? In *Civilization and Its Discontents* Freud points out that this question is one that "touches the fate of humanity," and states that "it may be hoped [that there will be an accommodation] in the future of civilization, however much that civilization may oppress the life of the individual to-day" (Freud 1930a [1929], SE 21:96, 141). But given the constant and far-reaching instinctual renunciation that Freud sees as the very basis of society, there seems little possibility for such an accommodation.

Nonetheless, it is possible for an individual who obeys society's rules to derive some pleasure from impulses whose satisfaction is forbidden by society: he or she can attain substitute pleasures through aim inhibition, sublimation, reaction formation, etc. By doing what benefits society instead of engaging in socially unacceptable behavior, an individual will avoid the pain of social and superego censure and will experience the pleasure of social and superego approbation.

In fact, the pleasure principle may dictate that, all things considered, one should ordinarily follow society's rules. As Freud explains:

> In the developmental process of the individual, the programme of the pleasure principle, which consists in finding the satisfaction of happiness, is retained as the main aim. Integration in, or adaptation to, a human community appears as a scarcely avoidable condition which must be fulfilled before this aim of happiness can be achieved. (p. 140)

(Yet, Freud is quick to add, "if it [the achievement of the individual's happiness] could be done without that condition, it would perhaps be preferable" [p. 140].)

Freud's views on the relation of the individual to society provide further justification for calling his moral theory individualistic. I have already explained that it is individualistic in the sense of counseling a person to seek his or her own pleasure rather than that of other people. But it is also individualistic in the sense of positing a fundamental and seemingly irreconcilable conflict between the individual and society.

Some scholars argue that the opposition in Freud between the individual and society is not as stark as I have portrayed; they point to certain nonindividualistic elements in Freud's thought. Jeffrey Abramson, for example, finds in Freud "two rival teachings" about the relation of the individual to society:

> The first, more accessible teaching declares the tragic opposition between instinct and culture . . . . The second, more hidden and central testament of psychoanalysis is to the essential sociability of human nature—the primal need, present already in infants, for the love, affection, and company of others. (Abramson 1984, p. 8)

Abramson stresses the role that Eros plays in Freud's later writings, and sees this instinct toward union as a communitarian impulse that transcends individualism. While admitting that Freud does not develop the social implications of Eros (pp. 4–5), Abramson maintains that the implications are there nonetheless.

As I pointed out in chapter 4, Freud's theory of Eros is somewhat obscure. Eros includes the sexual and ego instincts, but is also a cosmic, "mythological" force aiming at the unity of all human beings, and, more broadly, at the unity of all living substance (Freud 1920g, SE 18:52, n. 1; Freud 1930a [1929], SE 21:122; Freud 1933b [1932], SE 22:211). Cosmic Eros instills in human beings both individualistic impulses (the sexual and ego instincts) and communitarian impulses (the urge toward union with others) (Freud 1930a [1929], SE 21:140). As I argued in chapter 4, inasmuch as Eros is a cosmic force it does not meet Freud's definition of instinct: it is not an endosomatic stimulus and does not seem to operate by causing tension in the individual. Hence the urge toward unity implanted in an individual human being is not, in the strict sense, an instinct at all. Moreover, Freud stresses that in its action on individual human beings, "the main accent" of Eros falls not on the communitarian urge, but "mostly on the egoistic [individualistic] urge" (p. 140).

It is important to bear in mind that not all desire for union with others should be attributed to the communitarian side of Eros; when union with others is desired as a means toward personal happiness, the desire is due to the individualistic dimension of Eros (see Freud 1930a [1929], SE 21:140). Indeed, when Abramson speaks of the "primal need" for the love and company of others, he is in fact pointing more to individualistic Eros than to communitarian Eros.

On the whole, then, Freud's instinct theory and the moral philosophy flowing from it can be classified fairly as individualism. While a communitarian strand is present is his later writings, it is less important than the individualism that pervades his thought, and inasmuch as communitarianism depends on a mythology of a cosmic Eros, it lies outside Freud's instinct theory strictly understood.[5]

To return to the program of individualistic hedonism: Is there a set of specific rules that every person should follow to maximize his or her pleasure? Given the complex relation of the individual to society and to the various groups within it, the manifold ways of achieving substitute satisfaction of one's desires, and the considerable differences in the psychic constitution of individuals, it is unrealistic to lay down hard-and-fast rules for maximizing pleasure. As Freud observes, "There is no golden rule which applies to everyone [in the search for pleasure]: every man must find out for himself in what particular fashion he can be saved" (p. 83).

Ironically, even if a person were always to choose the most pleasurable alternative in each situation, he or she would not, according to the psychoanalytic theory of human nature, be fully happy. For instincts are operative as long as a person is alive, and instincts by nature involve tension. Since tension is unpleasure and happiness is pleasure (pp. 76–77, 140), no one can be wholly happy when alive. Complete freedom from tension comes only with death (recall the theory of the death instinct)—and surely it is odd to call a dead person happy. Even the relative happiness that can be experienced in life involves a paradox. Since happiness (pleasure) comes from reducing tension, the amount of happiness one can experience is limited by the amount of unhappiness (tension, unpleasure) experienced beforehand. There cannot be great happiness without great prior pain, and moderate pain limits a person to moderate happiness. One is reminded here of Freud's well-known remark that psychotherapy accomplishes much if it transforms a neurotic's misery into "common unhappiness" (Freud and Breuer 1895d [1893–95], SE 2:305).

Despite the impossibility of fully carrying out the dictates of the pleasure principle and eliminating all tension, we must do the best we can to maximize our pleasure. As Freud remarks, "The programme of becoming happy, which the pleasure principle imposes on us, cannot be fulfilled; yet we must not—indeed, we cannot—give up our efforts to bring it nearer to fulfilment by some means or other" (Freud 1930a [1929], SE 21:83). It other words, we must follow the ethical principle of individualistic hedonism. As individualistic hedonists, we shall not avoid all unpleasure, but we shall, perhaps, release nearly as much tension as builds up inside us. And this, in Freud's view, is the best anyone can do.

To sum up this part of the chapter: Freud's sexual-ego instinct classification theory, like his general definition of instinct, leads to a moral philosophy of individualistic hedonism. But the individualistic hedonism of the sexual-ego schema is more specific since it identifies the two basic types of human impulse and, through various hypotheses about the transformation of these impulses, makes it possible to consider whether, in a given situation, one should satisfy the original impulse or a substitute desire.

The third and final approach to Freud's moral philosophy is based on his life-death instinct classification schema. Matters would be simplified if this approach, like the first two, led to a moral theory of individualistic hedonism. But the theories of cosmic and Eros and of the mysterious death instinct make for a more complex moral theory. Before considering the moral implications of the life and death instincts as a pair of equiprimordial impulses, it will be useful to examine each instinct separately.

The life instinct taken by itself does imply, for the most part, a philosophy of individualistic hedonism. The life instinct consists mainly of the sexual and ego instincts of Freud's original classification schema, and these instincts do lead to such a philosophy. The one new element included in the life instinct, added to the sexual and ego instincts, is the impulse to social union implanted by communitarian Eros—and it is this new element that complicates matters. In working out the moral theory implied by Freud's instinct theory, one could ignore this social impulse, since this impulse (as we have seen) does not really fit Freud's general concept of instinct. Indeed, one of the marks of an instinct is that its satisfaction produces pleasure, and Freud expressly states that the communitarian impulse can conflict with the individual's pursuit of pleasure (Freud 1930a [1929], SE 21:140–141). The impulse to unity instilled by Eros, that is to say, could be viewed as something extraneous to human nature.

If, however, communitarian Eros is viewed as a part of human nature, then the moral philosophy flowing from Freud's theory of the life instinct would go beyond individualistic hedonism. For the primary moral directive is to fulfill our nature, and in order to live in accordance with the life instinct it would be necessary for us not only to satisfy our sexual and ego instincts, but also the impulses of communitarian Eros. And to be communitarian is not only to transcend individualism, but to transcend hedonism as well, since communitarian actions will at times conflict with our goal of pleasure.

It is not clear whether Freud himself considers the desire for social union a part—or at least a very central part—of human nature. For he continues to maintain that what human beings ultimately seek is happiness (pleasure) (p. 76), and states that this aim is "pushed into the background" by the impulse implanted by communitarian Eros for union with all human beings. "It almost seems as if the creation of a great human community would be most successful if no attention had to be paid to the happiness of the individual" (p. 140).

There is more to Freud's final instinct classification theory, however, than just the life instinct; there is also the death instinct. Before determining the moral implications of the death instinct by itself, it will be helpful to examine the relationship between the death instinct and the pleasure principle.

When Freud introduces the hypothesis of the death instinct in *Beyond the Pleasure Principle* in 1920, he claims that the death instinct is not subject to the pleasure principle. He says that the compulsion to repeat (a manifestation of the death instinct) "overrides" the pleasure principle and is "independent" of it; the processes of the death instinct "take place in mental life independently of the pleasure principle" (Freud 1920g, SE 18:22, 32, 62).

Later on Freud seems to change his position and view the death instinct as subject to the pleasure principle after all. In 1926 he speaks of the "feelings of pleasure-unpleasure, in accordance with which the whole mental apparatus regulates its activity" (Freud 1926e, SE 20:200), and the death instinct, it seems safe to say, is a part of the mind's activity. Freud makes the same point in another 1926 publication: "The course of mental processes is automatically regulated by the *'pleasure-unpleasure principle'*" (Freud 1926f, SE 20:266, Freud's emphasis). And a few years later he asserts that "the pleasure principle . . . dominates the operation of the mental apparatus from the start" (Freud 1930a [1929], SE 21:76).

Freud, however, never acknowledges a change from the position he took in *Beyond the Pleasure Principle*. In fact, in 1937 we find him restating his initial view that the death instinct is independent of the pleasure principle:

If we take into consideration the total picture made up of the phenomena of masochism immanent in so many people, the negative therapeutic reaction and the sense of guilt found in so many neurotics, we shall no longer be able to adhere to the belief that mental events are exclusively governed by the

desire for pleasure. These phenomena are unmistakable in-
dications of the presence of a power in mental life which
we . . . trace back to the original death instinct of living matter. (Freud 1937c, SE 23:243)

The conclusion to be drawn here seems to be that Freud is
simply not sure whether the pleasure principle rules the death instinct or not. And such a conclusion finds support in a remark in
An Outline of Psycho-Analysis, written near the end of his life:
"It remains a question of the highest theoretical importance, and
one that has not yet been answered, when and how it is ever possible for the pleasure principle to be overcome" (Freud 1940a
[1938], SE 23:198).

Although Freud is not sure whether the death instinct *aims at*
pleasure, he does state that the satisfaction of the death instinct as
such does not seem to *bring* pleasure:

The question arises whether the satisfaction of purely
destructive instinctual impulses can be felt as pleasure,
whether pure destructiveness without any libidinal admixture
occurs. Satisfaction of the death instinct remaining in the ego
seems not to produce feelings of pleasure. (p. 154, n. 1)

What moral theory follows from the death instinct considered
by itself? To fulfill our nature by fulfilling our death instinct
would be an individualism, since we would following our own impulse for death. But it would not be a hedonism, since we would be
seeking something other than pleasure. Hedonism states that
pleasure is the only thing we should seek for its own sake, and the
doctrine of the death instinct implies that we should follow this instinct despite the fact that doing so does not produce feelings of
pleasure.

If we consider the death instinct in isolation from the life instinct, and accept the assumption that what we should do fundamentally is fulfill our nature, what moral precept can we infer
from the doctrine of the death instinct? How do we go about
fulfilling this impulse? One way is obvious: we should die. A moral

precept counseling us to seek death is admittedly not very attractive, but it does seem to be a philosophical implication of Freud's theory.

Dying is not the only way to satisfy our death instinct, however. If Freud is correct in his claim that we can divert our impulse to self-destruction onto other creatures, we can fulfill our death instinct by destroying other beings. This version of the moral principle is not very attractive either, but once again it seems to be a legitimate philosophical inference—and one which Freud himself acknowledges:

> Impeded aggressiveness [i.e., aggressiveness not deflected on external objects] seems to involve a grave injury [to the individual]. It really seems as though it is necessary for us to destroy some other thing or person in order not to destroy ourselves, in order to guard against the impulsion to self-destruction. A sad disclosure indeed for the moralist! (Freud 1933a [1932], SE 22:105)

The deep individualism of Freud's moral philosophy is especially apparent in this "sad disclosure."

So far we have examined the moral implications of the life instinct taken by itself and the death instinct taken by itself. But Freud's final instinct classification theory maintains that human nature contains both these instincts—forces within us "struggling with each other from the very first" (Freud 1920g, SE 18:61, n. 1). The question now is how we can live our life in a way that satisfies both impulses.

In one sense the two instincts are clearly incompatible. If we decide to follow the death impulse in its original, self-destructive form, we obviously cannot at the same time satisfy the life impulse. It would be possible, however, to satisfy the death instinct simultaneously with the life instinct if we divert the death instinct from our own person onto other beings. Such a life would be "a conflict and compromise" between the two opposing groups of instincts (Freud 1923b, SE 19:41).

While it is possible to seek a compromise between the life and death instincts, it is not clear why, on Freudian grounds, such a compromise would be desirable. Why try to seek a balance between the two types of impulses? Why not devote all one's energies to fulfilling the life instinct? Or why not focus exclusively on the death instinct, in either its self-destructive or its aggressive form? And if one does choose the death instinct, on what basis would one decide which form to follow? There seems to be no theoretical basis, in Freud, on which to answer these questions.

Freud's final instinct classification schema, then, leads to no clear-cut moral theory. The general tone of the moral philosophy implied by this schema remains one of individualistic hedonism, but the notion of communitarian Eros has certain non-individualistic and nonhedonistic implications, and the death instinct is nonhedonistic.

The aim of this chapter has been to draw out the moral philosophy implicit in Freud's theory of instincts. The first two approaches to Freud's moral philosophy, i.e., those based on his general concept of instinct and on his sexual-ego classification schema, lead to a philosophy of individualistic hedonism. The third approach yields no definite moral theory, but has strong individualistic and hedonistic components. In light of all this, it seems fair to conclude that the best overall characterization of Freud's implicit moral philosophy is individualistic hedonism.

6

Individualism and
Group Psychology

THE main focus of Freud's research and writings is the psychology of the individual. His theory of instincts is a clear instance of an inquiry into the individual psyche. But Freud did not limit his attention to "individual psychology" (*Individualpsychologie*); he also took an interest in "group psychology" (*Massenpsychologie*), and in 1921 published a book entitled *Group Psychology and the Analysis of the Ego* (Freud 1921c). Here he examines the psychological characteristics of groups and discusses the historical origin of the moral regulations governing groups.

The views that Freud expounds in *Group Psychology and the Analysis of the Ego* and related works (principally *Totem and Taboo* [Freud 1912–13] and *Moses and Monotheism* [Freud 1939a (1934–38)]) in certain ways pose a challenge to my thesis in chapter

5 that Freud's moral philosophy is fundamentally individualistic. The present chapter sets forth Freud's views on group psychology and argues that these views are, for the most part, consistent with the individualism of his doctrine of instincts.

In *Group Psychology and the Analysis of the Ego*, Freud explains certain phenomena of group psychology in terms of libido theory and a historical hypothesis about a "primal horde" of human beings. He describes the subject matter of group psychology as "the individual man as a member of a race, of a nation, of a caste, of a profession, of an institution, or as a component part of a crowd of people who have been organized into a group at some particular time for some definite purpose" (Freud 1921c, SE 18:70). The relationships of an individual to the members of his or her family, and to other especially important persons, would fall more within the realm of individual psychology than group psychology (pp. 69–70).

When individuals join together and act as members of a group, their affective and intellectual processes often undergo remarkable changes (see pp. 72–81). The individual's "liability to affect becomes extraordinarily intensified, while his intellectual ability is markedly reduced, both processes being evidently in the direction of an approximation to the other individuals in the group" (p. 88). Freud seeks to explain these changes in terms of libido, "the energy . . . of those instincts which have to do with all that may be comprised under the word 'love'" (p. 90). There must be some force that binds members of a group together, and Freud will argue that the force must be love (Eros). "To what power could this feat be better ascribed than to Eros, which holds together everything in the world?" (p. 92).

Human feelings towards strangers usually contain an element of intolerance; an individual feels that the stranger's differences from him- or herself imply a criticism and a demand for change. But when a group forms, "the whole of this intolerance vanishes, temporarily or permanently, within the group" (p. 102). Since intolerance of others is rooted in love of self, and "love for oneself knows only one barrier—love for others," we can conclude that the overcoming of self-love in group psychology is caused by love for the other members of the group (p. 102). To the objection that the explanation for such tolerance could simply be collaboration in a common task, Freud responds that the tolerance outlasts the achievement of the task, and that the libidinal ties that result from collaboration go beyond the merely profitable (pp. 102–103).

The libidinal bonds among members of a group arise in part through the psychic mechanism of identification. To identify with someone means to take someone else as a model (either wholly or in part) and to shape one's own ego accordingly (pp. 105–106; Freud 1933a [1932], SE 22:63). In groups that have a leader, the members identify in some way with the leader, whom they internalize as their ego ideal. In this way group members come to have the same ego ideal, and as a result they identify with one another. As Freud puts it, the libidinal constitution of groups arises when "a number of individuals . . . have put one and the same object in the place of their ego ideal and have consequently identified themselves with one another in their ego" (Freud 1921c, SE 18:116; see p. 108).

Freud compares modern groups to the very first form of human society—which Freud hypothesizes to have been the "primal horde" (*Urhorde*). A primal horde is a group "ruled over despotically by a powerful male" (p. 122). Freud refers us to his original discussion of this topic in *Totem and Taboo*, where he describes a primal horde as a group with "a violent and jealous father who keeps all the females for himself and drives away his sons as they grow up" (Freud 1912–13, SE 13:141).

Freud credits Charles Darwin with first introducing the hypothesis of a primal horde (pp. 125, 141; Freud 1921c, SE 18:122). In *The Descent of Man* Darwin speculates that the social structure of primitive human beings may have been like that presently found among gorillas. Gorillas live in bands (Darwin does not use the term "horde"), and each band has one adult male with several females to himself. When the young males grow up, there is a contest for mastery, in which the winner kills or drives out the other males and takes over as head of the community (Darwin 1871, 2:362–363).

By jealously keeping all the women to himself, the primal human father prevented his sons from directly satisfying their sexual instincts. As a consequence, the sons rechanneled their libido into emotional ties with one another and with their father; the primal father "forced [his sons], so to speak, into group psychology" (Freud 1921c, SE 18:124).

The primal human horde, Freud explains, is similar in important respects to modern groups with a leader. In both cases there is

> an individual of superior strength among a troop of equal companions . . . , the dwindling of the conscious individual personality, the focusing of thoughts and feelings in a common direction, the predominance of the affective side of the mind and of unconscious psychical life, the tendency to the immediate carrying out of intentions as they emerge. (p. 122)

These similarities lead Freud to see modern groups as a revival of the primal horde: "Just as primitive man survives potentially in every individual, so the primal horde may arise once more out of any random collection; in so far as men are habitually under the sway of group formation we recognize in it the survival of the primal horde" (p. 123).

In *Totem and Taboo* Freud explains how morality arose from the association of brothers in the primal horde. The brothers who had been driven out of the horde by their father joined together and did what each one desired to do, but was unable to do individually: they killed and devoured their father. They killed him because he had "presented such a formidable obstacle to their craving for power and their sexual desires"; they devoured him because he was their envied model, and by eating him "they accomplished their identification with him, and each one of them acquired a portion of his strength" (Freud 1912-13, SE 13:141-143).

After carrying out this momentous deed, the sons began to feel the love and admiration for their father that had coexisted with their hatred of him; once their hatred had been satisfied by the act of murder, "the affection which had all this time been pushed under was bound to make itself felt" (p. 143). The feelings

of affection caused a sense of guilt, and guilt led the sons to pro-
hibit the killing of the animal they had chosen as a symbol and
substitute for their father—the totem. Guilt also caused the sons to
renounce the fruits of their murder: they gave up their sexual claim
to the women of the horde. Such, according to Freud, is the origin
of the two fundamental taboos of totemism (which correspond to
the two repressed wishes of the Oedipus complex), the killing of
the totem and incest. And these two taboos constitute the beginning of human morality (pp. 143–144; See Freud 1939a [1934–38],
SE 23:82.)[1]

In *Civilization and Its Discontents* Freud relates the moral
regulations of totemism to the superego and to the process of identification. The sons in the primal horde both hated and loved their
father, and it was this ambivalence that led to remorse: "After
their hatred had been satisfied by their act of aggression, their love
came to the fore in their remorse for the deed." Through the
mechanism of identification, their love for their father established
the superego. The superego received the father's power, "as
though as a punishment for the deed of aggression they had carried out against him, and it [the superego] created the restrictions
which were intended to prevent a repetition of the deed" (Freud
1930a [1929], SE 21:132). And it was the superego that issued the
taboos against killing and incest.

Freud explains in *Totem and Taboo* that the prohibition
against incest had a great practical advantage for the horde. While
each of the brothers wished to have all the women to himself, none
would have been powerful enough to subdue the others. The only
alternative to continual strife was to institute a law forbidding all
sexual relations with women in the horde. This enabled the
brothers to continue to exist as a unified group (Freud 1912–13, SE
13:144).

The emotional ties that had arisen among the brothers when
they were prevented by their father from directly satisfying their
sexual instincts continued to develop after they killed their father.
Eventually these bonds led them to sanctify their blood tie and to
emphasize the solidarity of all life within the horde. So the prohibition against killing, which originally applied only to the totem,

came to apply to all members of the horde. "In thus guaranteeing one another's lives, the brothers were declaring that no one of them must be treated by another as their father was treated by them" (p. 146).

In *Moses and Monotheism*, a much later work than *Totem and Taboo*, Freud returns to the subject of the historical origin of morality in the primal horde. He explains that after the sons had killed their father, there was a period in which they fought among themselves for their father's heritage. But they came to realize the dangers and uselessness of these struggles. This realization, along with

> a recollection of the act of liberation which they had accomplished together, and the emotional ties with one another which had arisen during the period of their expulsion, led at last to an agreement among them, a sort of a social contract . . . . [This involved] a *renunciation of instinct*, a recognition of mutual *obligations*, the introduction of definite *institutions* pronounced inviolable (holy)—that is to say, the beginnings of morality and justice. (Freud 1939a [1934–38], SE 23:82, Freud's emphasis)

Totem and Taboo had explained the origin of two moral rules among the brothers, the prohibition against killing members of the horde and the prohibition against incest. *Moses and Monotheism* discusses a third moral rule, "the granting of equal rights to all members of the fraternal alliance" (p. 119). This third regulation is "justified rationally by the necessity for delimiting the rights of society as against the individual, the rights of the individual as against society and those of individuals as against one another" (p. 122). Freud notes that the third rule differs in kind from the other two. The taboos against killing and incest "operate on the side of the father who has been got rid of: they carry on his will as it were." The institution of equal rights, by contrast, "disregards the father's will; it is justified by an appeal to the necessity of maintaining the new order which succeeded the father's removal" (p. 119).

Such, then, is the account of group psychology and the historical origin of morality that Freud gives in *Group Psychology and the Analysis of the Ego, Totem and Taboo*, and *Moses and Monotheism*.[2] We may now turn to the question of whether this account is compatible with the individualism of Freud's theory of instincts. Are the affectionate ties that exist among members of groups based on something other than self-interest? Does Freud's account of the origin of morality imply that human beings transcend individualism when following moral regulations? Let us consider each question in turn.

The affection that an individual may feel toward members of his or her group may seem to have a deeper basis than self-interest, but Freud's libido theory indicates otherwise. A person's libido aims primarily at sexual union with others (Freud 1921c, SE 18:90), but usually this aim cannot, of course, be directly realized. Affectionate bonds develop among members of a group as a substitute for direct sexual satisfaction. These bonds are "love instincts which have been diverted from their original aims" (p. 103). This diverting takes place through the psychic mechanism of aim inhibition. And aim inhibition, as I argued in the previous chapter, is individualistic because it is chosen (consciously or unconsciously) as a substitute for direct sexual satisfaction.

Freud explains how aim inhibition was operative in the group psychology of the primal horde:

> The primal father had prevented his sons from satisfying their directly sexual impulsions; he forced them into abstinence and consequently into the emotional ties with him and with one another which could arise out of their impulsions that were inhibited in their sexual aim. He forced them, so to speak, into group psychology. (p. 124)

Libidinal ties among members of groups are based not only on aim inhibition, but on identification as well. As we have seen, members of groups with a leader develop affectionate ties with one another because they all identify with the leader. Is the process of identification, like aim inhibition, individualistic? While Freud does not directly address this question, the answer seems affirmative.

The reason one identifies with another person is one's desire to be like that person. The sons in the primal horde identified with their father because they envied him (Freud 1912–13, SE 13:142). A young boy identifies with his father because "he would like to grow like him and be like him, and take his place everywhere" (Freud 1921c, SE 18:105). And why does someone desire to be like another person? Freud would probably say that being like the other person offers a prospect of more fully satisfying one's sexual and/or ego instincts. If the sons in the primal horde were like their father, they would be able to satisfy their sexual desires with the women in the horde; if a young boy were like his father, he would have his mother to himself, and would not have to fear punishment from his father. And because the sexual and ego instincts are individualistic (as I argued in the previous chapter), identification is also. So it seems fair to say that group ties based on this psychic mechanism are individualistic in nature.

Since sexual and ego instincts are at the basis of both individual psychology and group psychology, the distinction between these two fields of investigation is not as great as it first appears. As Freud states in his introduction to *Group Psychology and the Analysis of the Ego*, the distinction

> loses a great deal of its sharpness when it is examined more closely. It is true that individual psychology is concerned with the individual man and explores the paths by which he seeks to find satisfaction of his instinctual impulses; but only rarely and in certain exceptional conditions is individual psychology in a position to disregard the relations of this individual to others. In the individual's mental life someone else is invariably involved, as a model, as an object, as a helper, as an opponent; and so from the very first individual psychology, in this extended but entirely justifiable sense of the words, is at the same time social [group] psychology as well. (p. 69)

We may now turn to the question of whether the historical origin of morality as described by Freud implies that human beings in their social relationships transcend individualism. In Freud's account of the primal horde, do the moral regulations established by the brothers have a nonindividualistic basis?

As we have seen, human morality began when the brothers, after killing their father, established prohibitions against killing and against sexual relations with women of the horde. The reason the brothers instituted these taboos was the remorse they felt for killing their father. This remorse was due to love—the brothers' love for their father that had coexisted with their hatred of him. It was this love that led, through the process of identification, to the establishment of the superego. And it was the superego that forbade killing and incest.

Is the love that lay at the basis of the brothers' remorse, and thus at the basis of the two taboos and of human morality in general, itself individualistic? Freud explains in *Group Psychology and the Analysis of the Ego* that the nucleus of all forms of love, including love for parents, is "sexual love with sexual union as its aim" (p. 90). And sexual love is based on the individualistic sexual instinct. So, since the taboos are based on remorse, and remorse on love, it follows that the taboos are fundamentally individualistic.

In addition to the taboos against killing and incest, the brothers adopted a regulation granting equal rights to everyone in the horde. This rule may seen nonindividualistic, but it was ultimately grounded in self-interest. Freud explains that the brothers instituted equal rights out of "the necessity for permanently maintaining the new order which succeeded the father's removal. Otherwise a relapse into the earlier state would have become inevitable" (Freud 1939a [1934–38], SE 23:119; see p. 122). The reason a relapse would have been undesirable is precisely because it would have been contrary to the self-interest of each of the brothers.

In *Civilization and Its Discontents* Freud again gives an individualistic explanation of the origin of moral rules. Civilization began when human beings first attempted to regulate their social relationships; before such regulation

> the physically stronger man would decide [social relationships] in the sense of his own interests and instinctual impulses . . . . Human life in common is only made possible when a majority comes together which is stronger than any separate individual and which remains united against all separate individuals. The power of this community is then set up as 'right' in opposition to the power of the individual, which is condemned as 'brute force'. (Freud 1930a [1929], SE 21:95)

While it is true that individuals who join a community and follow its regulations must renounce certain instinctual satisfactions, the vast majority of individuals live a more pleasurable life in a community than they would under the rule of the physically stronger. Indeed, outside society even someone physically strong is in danger of being overpowered by someone stronger still.

The renunciation of instinctual satisfaction required by life in society gives another advantage to the weak and strong alike: by working together in society human beings can make great strides in defending themselves against the perils of nature. In *The Future of an Illusion* Freud identifies this as the principal benefit of civilization:

> How short-sighted . . . to strive for the abolition of civilization! What would then remain would be a state of nature, and that would be far harder to bear. It is true that nature would not demand any restrictions of instinct from us . . . , but she has her own particularly effective method of restricting us. She destroys us—coldly, cruelly, relentlessly . . . It was precisely because of these dangers with which nature threatens us that we came together and created civilization. (Freud 1927c, SE 21:15)

According to Freud, then, the regulations that govern members of a civilization clearly have an individualistic basis: the reason individuals join together in societies is to defend themselves against the aggression of more powerful individuals and to protect themselves against the forces of nature.

The biggest challenge to the claim that Freud's implicit theory is individualistic comes not from his views on affectionate ties among group members or from his account of the origin of morality, but from his doctrine of Eros. In *Group Psychology and the Analysis of the Ego* Freud incorporates Eros into his libido theory. Libido is the energy behind love in all its forms, and love in this broad sense is synonymous with Eros, the uniting force "which holds together everything in the world" (Freud 1921c, SE 18:92).

In *Civilization and Its Discontents* Freud explains in greater detail how Eros aims at unity. There he describes civilization as

> a process in the service of Eros, whose purpose is to combine single human individuals, and after that families, then races, peoples and nations, into one great unity, the unity of mankind. Why this has to happen, we do not know; the work of Eros is precisely this. These collections of men are to be libidinally bound to one another. Necessity alone, the advantages of work in common, will not hold them together. (Freud 1930a [1929], SE 21:122)

Freud goes on to explain that Eros is a cosmic force that plays a role both in the life of an individual and in the development of a civilization. He seems to view Eros as an entity in its own right, which has aims both for individuals and for civilization as such. Eros has a twofold influence both with respect to the individual and with respect to civilization: individualistic and communitarian ("egotistic" and "altruistic" in Freud's terminology). Individualistic Eros aims at the happiness (pleasure) of individual human beings, whereas communitarian Eros aims at the union of all human beings (p. 140).

With respect to the individual, the individualistic aspect of Eros exerts a stronger influence than the communitarian aspect: "In the developmental process of the individual, the programme of the pleasure principle, which consists in finding the satisfaction of happiness, is retained [by Eros] as the main aim." But communitarian Eros is also present, instilling in the individual an "urge toward union with others in the community" (p. 140).

As a force in the development of civilization, communitarian Eros almost completely overshadows individualistic Eros:

> Here by far the most important thing is the aim of creating a unity out of the individual human beings. It is true that the aim of happiness is still there, but it is pushed into the background. It almost seems as if the creation of a great human community would be most successful if no attention had to be paid to the happiness of the individual. (p. 140)

While Freud's notion of Eros as a force in civilization as such (i.e., civiliation as something more than the sum of the individuals comprising it) is a philosophically interesting one, we need not pursue it here. The question about individualism we are examining in this chapter refers to Eros as a force in the individual. And with regard to the individual, the presence of communitarian Eros in each human being seems to indicate that Freud's moral philosophy goes beyond individualism. For if my assumption is correct that to be moral means to fulfill our nature, and if communitarian Eros is a part of our nature, then it would seem that we should follow the dictates of communitarian Eros.

The moral situation, however, is complicated by the fact that the urges implanted in us by communitarian Eros may come into conflict with the urges of individualistic Eros. What is good for our group as a whole may not be in our own best interest. What should we do in such a case? Should we pursue our own happiness, or should we sacrifice it in "the service of [communitarian] Eros" (p. 122)?

When there is such a conflict, part of our nature will be left unfulfilled no matter which type of Eros we follow. So the question is: which part should we leave unfulfilled, our individualistic or our communitarian dimension? According to Freud, individualistic Eros plays a much larger role in the individual than communitarian Eros: the "main aim" of Eros with respect to the individual is "the satisfaction of happiness," and the "main accent" of Eros in an individual is "on the egoistic urge" (p. 140). And since individualistic Eros for Freud plays an inherently stronger role in our nature than communitarian Eros, it seems that we would do best to subordinate the latter to the former in cases of conflict.

In light of all this, it seems fair to conclude that Freud's doctrine of Eros is more individualistic than communitarian, despite the presence of communitarian Eros in every individual. Nevertheless, it is clear from the tone of Freud's later writings that he takes the goal of communitarian Eros seriously, and that there is a communitarian dimension to his thought.

The tension between individualism and communitarianism in Freud's theory of Eros is another instance of the dualism that pervades his thought. The dualism in his late period is even more pronounced than the dualism in the earlier stages of his instinct classification theory. For in his late period there is not only the initial dualism of the life and death instincts, but a duality within the life instinct (Eros) itself: Eros implants urges both toward happiness (individualism) and toward union with others (communitarianism). The difference between the two dualisms with regard to moral theory is that the life-death dualism yields no moral directive because the two instincts seem equally strong, whereas the individualism-communitarianism dualism seems to imply, ultimately, an individualism because the urge implanted by Eros for happiness predominates over the urge implanted by Eros for furthering community. (Whether individualistic or communitarian Eros will prevail in the course of human history would seem to be in the hands of cosmic Eros itself.)

The hypotheses Freud sets forth in *Group Psychology and the Analysis of the Ego*, *Totem and Taboo*, and *Moses and Monotheism* are, then, for the most part compatible with the individualism of his theory of instincts. Affectionate ties among members of groups arise from aim inhibition and identification, and these processes are individualistic. Moral regulations were instituted partly because of remorse, which is grounded in the sexual instinct, and partly because such regulations were in the best self-interest of the individuals comprising the group. The chief non-individualistic strand in Freud's doctrine of group psychology is the communitarian dimension of Eros. But in the end this communitarianism seems to be subordinate to the impulses of individualistic Eros impelling the individual to seek happiness.

Instincts are for Freud "the deepest essence of human nature," and this view of human nature leads to a moral philosophy. If to be moral means to fulfill our nature, and if our nature consists essentially of instincts, then we should live our lives in a way that satisfies our instinctual impulses as fully as possible. This moral philosophy is individualistic, and since the satisfaction of instincts is, according to Freud, the source of pleasure, it is a hedonism as well. Whether individualistic hedonism is a feasible moral philosophy is a difficult but important question—and one beyond the scope of this book. But those who accept Freud's doctrine of instincts should be aware of the moral philosophy to which it leads.

Freud's Instinct Classification Theory:
Three Stages or Four?

In Part One I distinguished three stages in Freud's continuing attempt to classify the basic human instincts: (1) his original theory of a sexual-ego dualism (1899–1914), (2) the period in which he maintained his sexual-ego theory despite the monistic implications of his analysis of narcissism (1914–1920), and (3) his final theory of a life-death dualism (1920–1939). This interpretation of Freud's views on the classification of instincts agrees with that given by Ernest Jones in his 1936 article "Psycho-Analysis and the Instincts" (Jones 1936). There are two authors, however, who argue for four stages in the development of Freud's instinct classification theory.

Edward Bibring maintains that Freud arrived at his final life-death theory through a series of four steps: (1) a sexual-ego dualism (until 1914), (2) a dualism of libidinal ego instincts and nonlibidinal ego instincts (1914–1915), (3) the removal of aggressive impulses from the category of sexual instincts and their placement under the ego instincts (1915–1920), and (4) the separation of the aggressive impulses from the ego instincts (1920 onward)—the step that gave rise to Freud's culminating life-death theory (Bibring 1941 [based on lectures given in 1934]).

Rose Edgcumbe's analysis agrees essentially with Bibring's (though she makes no reference to his article). Her four stages are:

(1) a sexual-dualism (implicit from 1894 to 1897, explicit from 1897 to 1911), (2) a dualism of libidinal ego instincts and nonlibidinal ego instincts (1911–1914), (3) the moving of aggressive impulses from the sexual instincts to the ego instincts (1915–1920); and (4) a dualism of the life and death instincts, with the sexual instincts placed under the former category and the aggressive instincts under the latter (1920–1939) (Edgcumbe 1970).

Edgcumbe differs from Bibring only in distinguishing implicit and explicit phases of the first stage, in assigning different dates to the second stage, and in combining Bibring's fourth step with the general life-death theory that Bibring sees as emerging from this step. These differences are minor, and need not concern us here.

I quite agree with Bibring and Edgcumbe that Freud began with a sexual-ego dualism and ended with a life-death dualism, but do not accept their thesis that Freud made two revisions in his instinct theory before formulating the life-death theory. As I explained in chapters 3 and 4, I hold that Freud maintained his original sexual-ego dualism from 1914 to 1920, despite the apparently monistic implications of his 1914 essay "On Narcissism" (Freud 1914c), and abandoned his sexual-ego dualism only when he was able to replace it with the more sweeping life-death dualism set forth in *Beyond the Pleasure Principle* (Freud 1920g).

Bibring and Edgcumbe claim that Freud first modified his sexual-ego theory by positing a new dualism of libidinal and nonlibidinal ego instincts (their Stage 2), and then removed aggressive impulses from the sexual instincts and included them in the ego instincts (their Stage 3). But I find no solid evidence in Freud for either of these intermediate stages. Let us examine each one in turn.

Bibring and Edgcumbe maintain that when Freud realized that his analysis of the phenomenon of narcissism seemed to reduce his sexual-ego dualism to a monism, he salvaged an instinctual dualism by dividing the ego instincts into libidinal and nonlibidinal impulses. They claim to find support for this distinction in Freud's essay "On Narcissism." Bibring argues as follows:

> [Freud] asserted that what was known as egoism [the ego in-
> stincts] has two components, a libidinal-narcissistic compo-
> nent and a non-libidinal component. Narcissism, as he wrote,
> is only 'the libidinal complement to the egoism of the instinct
> of self-preservation, a measure of which may justifiably be
> attributed to every living creature.' Originally, these two
> components were undifferentiated. (Bibring 1941, p. 109)

The crucial word in Bibring's argument is "only"; if narcissism is *only* the libidinal complement to the ego instincts, then it
does seem to follow that there are *non*libidinal ego instincts as
well. But Freud's text does not contain or imply the word "only."
Freud's full sentence is: "Narcissism in this sense [as a part of the
regular course of human sexual development] would not be a
perversion, but the libidinal complement to the egoism of the instinct of self-preservation, a measure of which may justifiably be
attributed to every living creature" (Freud 1914c, SE 14:73–74).
Freud here is not trying to distinguish libidinal and nonlibidinal ego instincts, but simply saying that ego instincts have
a libidinal aspect; indeed, it is the very fact that ego instincts
have a libidinal aspect that causes Freud to question his
sexual-ego dualism (for if the ego instincts are originally libidinal [sexual], the sexual-ego distinction would be derivative,
not primordial).

Edgcumbe, like Bibring, cites the above text from "On Narcissism" as evidence for a bifurcation of the ego instincts into
libidinal and nonlibidinal impulses. Unlike Bibring, she does not
introduce the quotation with the misleading word "only"; she
simply says that "he [Freud] speaks of narcissism as: ' . . . the
libidinal complement to the egoism of the instinct of self-
preservation . . . '" (Edgcumbe 1970, p. 37). While her citation is
accurate, it does not constitute evidence for a division between
libidinal and nonlibidinal ego instincts; the quotation merely states
that the phenomenon of narcissism shows that the ego instincts
have a libidinal component.

Bibring and Edgcumbe interpret the quoted passage from "On Narcissism" as Freud's solution to the problem of instinctual monism raised by his analysis of narcissism. But this passage occurs at the *beginning* of the essay (in the second paragraph), before Freud has even raised the problem of monism. It would be odd for Freud (or anyone else) to present the solution to a problem before even stating what the problem is.

To further support their claim that Freud posits a class of nonlibidinal ego instincts, Bibring and Edgcumbe assert that Freud uses the term "interest" ("ego-interest") to denote these instincts (Bibring 1941, pp. 103, 109; Edgcumbe 1970, p. 27). But they give no evidence for their assertion. In point of fact, Freud does not even mention the concept of interest when discussing the problem of monism in "On Narcissism"; he uses it only later on in the essay, when discussing the relation of narcissism to organic disease and to hypochondria (Freud 1914c, SE 14:82–84). And in this discussion "interest" clearly refers to the energy behind all the ego instincts; it is correlative to libido, which is the energy behind all the sexual instincts (thus Freud's phrases "libido and ego-interest" and "both interest and libido" [pp. 82, 83]). This is the same meaning "interest" has in Freud's later writings (e.g., Freud 1916–17 [1915–17], SE 16:414; Freud 1917d [1915], SE 14:235). As Strachey comments, "The term is regularly used . . . to distinguish self-preservative forces from the libido" (Strachey, SE 16:414–415, n. 2).

Perhaps the strongest reason for rejecting Bibring and Edgcumbe's claim that Freud in "On Narcissism" posits a dualism between libidinal and nonlibidinal ego instincts is the following. After admitting that his analysis of narcissism seems to imply an instinctual monism, Freud proceeds to give several arguments "in favor of there having been from the first a distinction between the sexual and . . . ego-instincts" (Freud 1914c, SE 14:78). The plain meaning of these arguments is that despite the fact that narcissism points toward a monism, Freud nevertheless holds on to his original sexual-ego dualism. As I argued in chapter 3, Freud is unwilling to abandon his original dualistic theory until he can replace it with a more fundamental dualism—which he does in 1920 when he puts forth his life-death theory.

A final point. If Freud had meant to propose in "On Narcissism" a revision of his long-standing instinct classification theory, one would expect him to have made it clear that he was doing so, as he did when introducing his new life-death dualism in *Beyond the Pleasure Principle* (Freud 1920g, SE 18:53). But "On Narcissism" contains no clear evidence of a revision—for the simple reason, in my view, that there is no revision.

The third stage in Freud's instinct classification theory, according to Bibring and Edgcumbe, occurred when Freud removed aggressive impulses from the category of the sexual instincts and placed them under the ego instincts. Bibring and Edgcumbe argue that Freud made this revision in his 1915 essay "Instincts and Their Vicissitudes" (Freud 1915c).

In this essay, according to Bibring, Freud "gave the aggressive trends an independent status *vis-à-vis* the libidinal currents and classed them as belonging to the ego instincts"; he "ascribe[d] the characteristic of aggressiveness . . . to the ego instincts" (Bibring 1941, pp. 110, 112). Bibring does not cite any specific passages from "Instincts and Their Vicissitudes" to support his interpretation, but the chief text he has in mind seems to be the following:

> The ego hates, abhors and pursues with intent to destroy all objects which are a source of unpleasurable feeling for it . . . . Indeed, it may be asserted that the true prototypes of the relation of hate are derived not from sexual life, but from the ego's struggle to preserve and maintain itself . . . . Hate, as a relation to objects, is older than love . . . . It always remains in an intimate relation with the self-preservative instincts. (Freud 1915c, SE 14:138–139)

The above passage is the principal one quoted by Edgcumbe in support of her claim for the alleged third stage in Freud's instinct classification theory, the stage in which "aggression, previously considered to be a component of the sexual instinct, [is] ascribed . . . to the non-libidinal ego instincts" (Edgcumbe 1970, p. 27; passage cited on p. 40). But it is hardly clear that this text constitutes a revision in Freud's instinct theory.

First, the passage is about hate, not aggression. Edgcumbe's argument rests on the assumption that these two terms are synonymous for Freud, but they are not. The most important difference is that for Freud aggression is an instinct, whereas hate is not. In "Instincts and Their Vicissitudes" Freud explicitly states that hate (like love) is not an instinct; "The attitudes of love and hate cannot be made use of for the relations of *instincts* to their objects, but are reserved for the relations of the *total ego* [total self] to objects" (Freud 1915c, SE 14:137, Freud's emphasis). (Bibring goes even farther than Edgcumbe, equating not only aggression and hate [Bibring 1941, p. 113], but aggression and sadism [p. 112].) Since hate is not an instinct, a new hypothesis on the relation of hate to the ego instincts would not constitute a new theory of instinct classification.

Second, Bibring and Edgcumbe's thesis about Freud's third stage assumes that prior to 1915 Freud had clearly classified aggression as a sexual instinct. But as I pointed out in chapter 4, Freud was unsure at this time whether to consider aggression a sexual instinct, an ego instinct, or a characteristic of both. So even if Freud did, in 1915, decide to place aggression in the category of the ego instincts, this decision should not be considered a major revision in his instinct theory. But it is not even clear that Freud made such a decision, since (to return to my previous point) the passage is about the relation of *hate* to the ego instincts, not aggression: to reclassify the former is not necessarily to reclassify the latter. Moreover, the fact that hate (or aggression) has an "intimate relation" to the ego instincts does not necessarily mean that hate (or aggression) is to be wholly included in them.

Finally, I raise again the point that if Freud had intended to make a revision in his instinct theory, one would expect him to have done so explicitly and unequivocally. But no such explicit statement is to be found in "Instincts and Their Vicissitudes." Bibring is quite aware of this fact; when introducing the alleged third stage in Freud's instinct theory, he remarks that it has "for the most part been overlooked in psycho-analytical writings" (Bibring 1941, p. 103). The reason for its being overlooked, I submit, is not hard to find.

The evidence, then, points to three stages in the development of Freud's views on the classification of instincts, not four. Ernest Jones got it right in 1936, and was not guilty of oversight.

Chapter 1

1. "Instinct" is James Strachey's translation in the *Standard Edition* of Freud's term *Trieb* (see Strachey, SE 1:xxiv-xxvi). Since *Trieb* derives from *trieben*, "to drive, push, propel," a better translation may be "drive" (Bettelheim 1983, pp. 103–104) or "instinctual drive" (Schur 1967, p. 25, n. 1; Moore and Fine 1968, pp. 55–57). Since I generally quote from Strachey's translations, for the sake of simplicity I use "instinct" throughout the book.

As Strachey points out, in those few cases in which Freud uses the German *Instinkt*, he usually means it in the sense of instinct in animals (Strachey, SE 1:xxv).

2. "Unpleasure" is Strachey's translation of *Unlust*. While "pain" would be a more natural translation, "unpleasure" is a reminder that *Unlust* is in German the negation of *Lust* (pleasure). See Strachey, SE 1:xxvi.

3. Jones is thus mistaken in his claim that "Instincts and Their Vicissitudes" (published in 1915) constitutes "the first time Freud wrote anything about the nature of instincts" (Jones 1936, p. 276).

4. "Cathect" is a term coined by Strachey to translate Freud's *besetzen*. In ordinary German, *besetzen* means "to occupy (an area)." Strachey derived "cathect" from the Greek *katechein*, which also means "to occupy (an area)." To cathect an idea with

111

energy is to attach energy to it, to invest it with energy. The noun *Besetzung* is rendered "cathexis," from the Greek *kathexis*. See Strachey, SE 3:63, n. 2.

Chapter 4

1. Freud points out that recurring traumatic dreams constitute an exception to his thesis in *The Interpretation of Dreams* that all dreams are wish fulfillments (Freud 1920g, SE 18:32).

2. Note that since the sexual instincts contradict Freud's tentative hypothesis that the repetition compulsion characterizes all instincts, Freud has to reject the definition of instinct derived from that hypothesis, namely, "an urge inherent in organic life to restore an earlier state of things" (Freud 1920g, SE 18:36). Some authors, e.g., Max Schur, have mistakenly seen this as a "new definition of instinct" intended by Freud to replace the definition given in "Instincts and Their Vicissitudes" (Schur 1967, pp. 165, 169–170).

3. To contrast the death instinct with Eros, some authors refer to it as "Thanatos" (the Greek word for death). Freud himself, however, does not use this term.

4. Since the ego instincts are part of the life instincts, Chessick overstates the case when he claims that with the introduction of the life-death instinct classification theory Freud "abandons the notion of the ego instincts entirely" (Chessick 1980, p. 260).

5. Cosmic Eros as a force in the individual is discussed more fully in chapter 6, in the context of group psychology.

Chapter 5

1. More recently, Ilham Dilman has argued that although hedonism is a legitimate philosophical implication of Freud's

stated views on human nature, this implication is " 'philosophical froth' [and] not an essential part of what [Freud] had to say." Dilman regards a nonhedonistic reading of Freud as "more consonant with the spirit of psycho-analysis" (Dilman 1983, p. 3). But except for certain remarks Freud makes about Eros in his late period (which I discuss in chapter 6), both the letter and the spirit of his psychoanalytic theory seem quite hedonistic.

2. The philosophical position I call "individualism" is more commonly known as "egoism." I have avoided the latter term because it would be confusing in a discussion of psychoanalysis, where "ego" and "ego instinct" are technical terms.

3. Initially Freud categorized reaction formation as a species of sublimation (Freud 1905d, SE 7:178, 238), but later came to view it as a separate process (Freud 1905d [1915 add.], SE 7:178, n. 2).

4. The phrase derives from Plautus, *Asinaria* II.4.88: *lupus est homo homini.*

5. The relation of individualism and communitarianism in Freud's later writings is discussed in greater detail in the following chapter.

Chapter 6

1. Freud notes in *Moses and Monotheism* that his account of the primal horde and the origin of morality is "enormously condensed." These events did not happen on a single occasion, but "covered thousands of years and [were] repeated countless times during that long period" (Freud 1939a [1934–38], SE 23:81).

2. For an account of various anthropological critiques of Freud's hypothesis of the primal horde, see Wallace 1983.

References

The abbreviation SE designates *The Standard Edition of the Complete Psychological Works of Sigmund Freud*, edited and translated by James Strachey, 24 vols., (London: The Hogarth Press and The Institute of Psycho-Analysis, 1953–74). Individual works from the SE cited in the text are listed chronologically, by the year of the first German edition. Different works published by Freud in the same year are distinguished by the lower-case letters assigned by Strachey in his complete listing of Freud's publications (SE 24:47–82). If Freud wrote a work prior to its year of publication, the date of composition follows in square brackets. (In the text of the book, square brackets also indicate a reference to a revised section of a work. For example, "Freud 1905d [1915 add.], SE 7:168" means that the passage cited was added by Freud to his 1915 edition of 1905d.)

Abramson, Jeffrey B. *Liberation and Its Limits: The Moral and Political Thought of Freud*. New York: Free Press, 1984.

Bettleheim, Bruno. *Freud and Man's Soul*. New York: Alfred A. Knopf, 1983.

Bibring, Edward. "The Development and Problems of the Theory of the Instincts." *The International Journal of Psychoanalysis* 22 (1941): 102–131.

Chessick, Richard D. *Freud Teaches Psychotherapy*. Indianapolis: Hackett Publishing Co., 1980.

References

Daley, James W. "Freud and Hedonism." *Journal of Value Inquiry* 1 (Winter 1967–68): 198–209.

Darwin, Charles. *The Descent of Man, and Selection in Relation to Sex.* 2 vols. London: John Murray, 1871.

Dilman, Ilham. *Freud and Human Nature.* Oxford: Basil Blackwell, 1983.

Edgcumbe, Rose. "The Development of Freud's Instinct Theory, 1894–1939." In *Basic Psychoanalytic Concepts on the Theory of Instincts*, pp. 23–49. Edited by Humberto Nagera. London: George Allen and Unwin, 1970.

Freud, Sigmund, and Breuer, Josef. *Studies on Hysteria.* SE 2:3–305. (1895d [1893–95])

Freud, Sigmund. *The Interpretation of Dreams.* SE 4: 1–338 and 5:339–621. (1900a [1899])

——. *The Psychopathology of Everyday Life: Forgetting, Slips of the Tongue, Bungled Actions, Superstitions and Errors.* SE 6:1–279. (1901b)

——. *Three Essays on the Theory of Sexuality.* SE 7:135–243. (1905d)

——. "Fragment of an Analysis of a Case of Hysteria." SE 7: 7–122. (1905e)

——. "Obsessive Actions and Religious Practices." SE 9:117–127. (1907b)

——. "'Civilized' Sexual Morality and Modern Nervous Illness." SE 9:181–204. (1908d)

——. "Analysis of a Phobia in a Five-Year-Old Boy." SE 10: 5–147. (1909b)

——. *Five Lectures on Psycho-Analysis.* SE 11:9–55. (1910a [1909])

———. *Leonardo da Vinci and a Memory of His Childhood.* SE 11:63–137. (1910c)

———. "A Special Type of Object Choice Made by Men" (*Contributions to the Psychology of Love I*). SE 11: 165–175. (1910h)

———. "The Psycho-Analytic View of Psychogenic Disturbance of Vision." SE 11:211–218. (1910i)

———. "'Wild' Psycho-Analysis." SE 11:221–227. (1910k)

———. "Formulations on the Two Principles of Mental Functioning." SE 12:218–226. (1911b)

———. "Psycho-Analytical Notes on an Autobiographical Account of a Case of Paranoia (Dementia Paranoides)." SE 12:9–79. (1911c [1910])

———. "On the Universal Tendency to Debasement in the Sphere of Love" (*Contributions to the Psychology of Love II*). SE 11:179–190. (1912d)

———. "Recommendations to Physicians Practicing Psycho-Analysis." SE 12:111–120. (1912e)

———. *Totem and Taboo: Some Points of Agreement Between the Mental Lives of Savages and Neurotics.* SE 13:1–161. (1912–13)

———. "The Claims of Psycho-Analysis to Scientific Interest." SE 13:165–190. (1913j)

———. "On Narcissicm: An Introduction." SE 14:73–102. (1914c)

———. "Thoughts for the Times on War and Death." SE 14:275–300. (1915b)

———. "Instincts and Their Vicissitudes." SE 14:117–140. (1915c)

References

————. "Repression." SE 14:146–158. (1915d)

————. "The Unconscious." SE 14:166–204. (1915e)

————. "Some Character-Types Met with in Psycho-Analytic Work." SE 14:311–333. (1916d)

————. *Introductory Lectures on Psycho-Analysis.* SE 15: 15–239 and 16:243–463. (1916–17 [1915–17])

————. "A Metapsychological Supplement to the Theory of Dreams." SE 14:222–235. (1917d [1915])

————. "Lines of Advance in Psycho-Analytic Therapy." SE 17: 159–168. (1919a [1918])

————. Introduction to *Psycho-Analysis and the War Neuroses.* SE 17:207–210. (1919d)

————. *Beyond the Pleasure Principle.* SE 18:7–64. (1920g)

————. *Group Psychology and the Analysis of the Ego.* SE 18: 69–153. (1921c)

————. "Two Encyclopedia Articles. (A) Psycho-Analysis; (B) The Libido Theory." SE 18:235–259. (1923a [1922])

————. *The Ego and the Id.* SE 19:12–59. (1923b)

————. "The Economic Problem of Masochism." SE 19:159–170. (1924c)

————. "The Dissolution of the Oedipus Complex." SE 19:173–179. (1924d)

————. *An Autobiographical Study.* SE 20:7–70. (1925d [1924])

————. "The Resistances to Psycho-Analysis." SE 19:213–224. (1925e [1924])

————. "Some Additional Notes on Dream-Interpretation as a Whole." SE 19:127–138. (1925i)

————. *Inhibitions, Symptoms and Anxiety.* SE 20:87–172. (1926d [1925])

————. *The Question of Lay Analysis: Conversations with an Impartial Person.* SE 12:183-250. (1926e)

————. "Psycho-Analysis." SE 20:263-270. (First published in English as an article in the 13th ed. of the *Encyclopaedia Britannica* [1926]) (1926f)

————. *The Future of an Illusion.* SE 21:5-56. (1927c)

————. *Civilization and Its Discontents.* SE 21:64-145. (1930a [1929])

————. *New Introductory Lectures on Psycho-Analysis.* SE 22:5-182. (1933a [1932])

————. "Why War?" SE 22:203-215. (1933b [1932])

————. Postscript to *An Autobiographical Study*, 2nd ed. SE 20:71-74. (1935a)

————. "Analysis Terminable and Interminable." SE 23:216-253. (1937c)

————. *Moses and Monotheism: Three Essays.* SE 23:7-137. (1939a [1934-38])

————. *An Outline of Psycho-Analysis.* SE 23:144-207. (1940a [1938])

———— and Breuer, Josef. "On the Theory of Hysterical Attacks." SE 1:151-154. (1940d [1892])

————. *Letters of Sigmund Freud.* Edited by Ernst L. Freud. Translated by Tania Stern and James Stern. New York: Basic Books, 1960.

————. *The Complete Letters of Sigmund Freud to Wilhelm Fliess, 1887-1904.* Translated and edited by Jeffrey Moussaieff Masson. Cambridge: Harvard University Press, 1985.

Jones, Ernest. "Psycho-Analysis and the Instincts." *The British Journal of Psychology* 26 (January 1936): 273-288.

References
___

———. *The Life and Work of Sigmund Freud*. 3 vols. New York: Basic Books, 1953, 1955, 1957.

Moore, Burness E., and Fine, Bernard D. *A Glossary of Psychoanalytic Terms and Concepts*. 2nd ed. New York: American Psychoanalytic Association, 1968.

Rieff, Philip. *Freud: The Mind of the Moralist*. 3rd ed. Chicago: University of Chicago Press, 1979. (1st ed., New York: Viking Press, 1959)

Schur, Max. *The Id and the Regulatory Principles of Mental Functioning*. New York: International Universities Press, 1967.

Wallace, Edwin R. *Freud and Anthropology: A History and Reappraisal*. New York: International Universities Press, 1983.

Wallach, Michael A., and Wallach, Lise. *Psychology's Sanction for Selfishness: The Error of Egoism in Theory and Therapy*. San Francisco: W. H. Freeman & Co., 1983.

Yankelovich, Daniel, and Barrett, William. *Ego and Instinct: The Psychoanalytic View of Human Nature—Revised*. New York: Random House, 1970.

Index